Allan King

Wings on Windermere
The history of the Lake District's forgotten flying boat factory

STRATUS

Table of contents

Published in Poland in 2008
by STRATUS s.c.
Po. Box 123,
27-600 Sandomierz 1, Poland
e-mail: office@mmpbooks.biz
for
Mushroom Model Publications,
36 Ver Road, Redbourn,
AL3 7PE, UK.
e-mail: rogerw@mmpbooks.biz
© 2008 Mushroom Model
Publications.
http://www.mmpbooks.biz

ISBN:
978-83-89450-82-1

Editor in chief
Roger Wallsgrove

Editorial Team
Bartłomiej Belcarz
Robert Pęczkowski
Artur Juszczak

Colour Drawings
Teodor Liviu Morusanu

DTP
Artur Bukowski

Printed by
Drukarnia Diecezjalna,
ul. Żeromskiego 4,
27-600 Sandomierz
tel. +48 (15) 832 31 92;
fax +48 (15) 832 77 87
www.wds.pl
marketing@wds.pl

PRINTED IN POLAND

On title page:

Launching: The first Windermere Sunderland DP176 touches the water for the first time. The front turret is winched back to allow a crewman to stand ready to catch the mooring, the two outer engines are running to provide steering and a drogue can be seen under the wing hanging from the galley window to give extra help with steering if needed.

Derek Hurst

Acknowledgements

No book of this type could be the product of just one person. There were a great many involved whose help ranged from giving freely of their time and knowledge to the support and encouragement needed to spend so many years on a single project.

I have tried to keep track of the many people who contributed but to any who are inadvertently missed off this list, my apologies and thanks for their help.

The project only ever really got off the ground because of two coauthors: Graham Coster and Derek Hurst both willingly allowed me to go on alone and Derek readily loaned photographs from his collection.

Many former workers at Shorts in Windermere allowed me to interview them, usually at length. They are: Mrs A M Burrow, Mrs E S V Cheals, Mr R Clayton, Marjorie. Crosland, Jim Dunlop, Stan Fearon, Jim Frearson, Vera George. Mr Gerrish, Joan Gibson, Jeff Gill, Sheila Gudgeon, Bill Harrison, Nick and Rita Holt, Mr M Jones, Elsie Kwaitkowski, Mrs Lavender, George Lidster, Llew Llewellyn, Olive Mayor, Eric Mitchinson, Richard Mooney, Mr W H Morgan, Stan O'Connor, Norman Parker, Eilene Satterthwaite, Eva Storrow, Issac Teasdale, Marjorie Winston and particularly Peter Greetham for his hospitality and loan of photographs from his father's collection.

Other help locally was generously given by: Mrs Anne Harrington, Angus and Lilly McKay, Peter Haslam, Harry Kissack and George Pattinson.

Many former RAF aircrew also gave valuable help with their recollections and information from their log books about Windermere built Sunderlands. I would like to thank: S/Ldr. E W Beer, Bill Campbell, Mr N Duke, Dick Dulieu, Ian Fraser, F/Lt K Harper, Mr Haynes, Andrew Hendrie, Captain Vic Hodgkinson, Mr M Hurt, Mr Hutchinson, Vic Kelly, John Land, Brian Landers, John Leeks, Dick Leese, Bernard Lyons, Jack Mansfield, W/Cdr Derek Martin, Gerry Morbey, Peter Naylor, Denis Rolph, Les Shaw, Bernard Smith, Peter Steiner, S/Ldr Fred Weaver and Bill Whiter.

Several squadron associations put me in contact with their members and I am grateful to: F/Lt John Bowland (201 Sqn) , Bill Balderson (210 Sqn), Eric Harrison (228 Sqn), Don Holloway (230 Sqn), Mrs. Jean Doern (422 Sqn), Jim Wright (423 Sqn), Barry Collins (88 Sqn), Ron Gadd (Air crew association), David Legg (Catalina Society) Geoff Guy (Indian Ocean Flying Boat Association),

Much other valuable assistance was given by: Barry Abraham, Chaz Bowyer, Peter Connon, Mrs J Brooke-Smith, John Gordon, John Hamlin, Norman Hull, Alexander Norton, Roy Perkins, Simon Shreeve, James Stewart, Harra Townsend, and holocaust survivor Mayer Hersh. Special thanks to Sally Beckett, daughter of John Lankester Parker for her hospitality and access to her father's papers; Ron Parsons for his insight into Shorts Brothers history; and Sunderland expert John Evans for access to his collections and his guidance; Celia King for help with research; Liz Rice and Trevor Avery for sharing information with their project; Catherine Kay and Michelle Oskoui for proof reading.

I would also like to thank the staff at the RAF Museum at Hendon, the National Archives, Kew and the Imperial War Museum, London and Hans Bredow at the U-boat Archive in Cuxhaven, Germany. I am also indebted to: the Air Historic Branch of the MoD, Albright and Wilson, Cumbria County Library Service, Cumbria Record Office, Kendal, Commonwealth War Graves Commission, Deutsches Schiffahrtsmuseum, Bremerhaven and the Royal New Zealand Air Force Museum, Christchurch.

Ready for Action: Two aircraft on the moorings at the north side of White Cross Bay.

Peter Greetham

Over Singapore: DP198 over Singapore, probably on one of the last flights in 1959.

Air Historic Branch

A late visitor

In the summer of 1990 crowds gathered on vantage points all around Windermere - any piece of ground with a good view of the lake attracted a crowd, the shoreline from Bowness to White Cross Bay had clumps of expectant people looking eagerly out across the strangely empty waters. A knot of people formed on Orrest Head.

Some took their boats out onto the lake but were shepherded by the police and warden speed boats into a long line on the eastern side - all facing into the centre of the lake.

With the runway cleared, the world's last airworthy Sunderland flying boat was ready to leave Windermere – probably never to return. Islander, a civilian conversion from the former military aircraft ML814, was at the time based at Southampton but had flown to Windermere four weeks before for the lake festival.

With the four engines fired up she taxied slowly away from her mooring off White Cross Bay and headed north.

From Queen Adelaide's Hill, just outside Bowness, the aircraft appeared small in the distance - dwarfed against the height of the mountains and the size of the lake. But the distance hid its true size. This double-decker aircraft with four huge 1,000 hp engines, provided its 15 man crew with bunks for sleeping, a galley for meals and even a flush toilet. With its heritage from the same design team who built the famous passenger and airmail carrying Empire Flying Boats, the Sunderland flying boats were giants, not just in size but also stature. They were the only four engined aircraft in RAF service at the start of World War II and one of the military's most sophisticated aircraft.

And they had been built in Windermere. Now the last one was leaving and everybody wanted to watch.

The crowds on the top of the hill had spread out, each moving to a clear spot for a view just as the sound of the engines being revved up reached us across the lake. The wide bow wave formed and then subsided as the aircraft started to rise from the water, but then she settled back into the water and slowed. She turned and headed north again.

Final departure: Islander, the only airworthy Sunderland leaves Windermere for the last time in July 1990.

Allan King

Moored up: At home among the yachts, Islander spent four weeks on the lake.

                 Allan King

Farewell flypast: Islander turns over Bowness Bay before heading north for an airshow appearance at Sunderland.

                 Allan King

Islander was reluctant to leave.

This aircraft was not a Windermere veteran - she had been built in Belfast at the Short and Harland factory where Shorts still have their works.[1] But the true home of the Sunderland was in Kent, at Rochester on the banks of the Medway where Short Brothers established their Seaplane Works during World War One. They became the leading company for floatplane and flying boat design.

The monoplane design and sheer size was radical in 1933 when the first Sunderland flew.[2] Built in parallel to the Empire boats used for airmail and passenger routes to South Africa and India, Short Brothers produced a superb aircraft to meet the government's requirements for a maritime patrol and antisubmarine aircraft.

Windermere was one of four sites to build the Sunderland under expansion plans that also sought to spread production around the country and minimise the risk of damage from German bombing.

When, 45 years later, the only airworthy aircraft was brought to Windermere for the lake festival, a continual stream of visitors wanted to be taken out on launches to see inside. Of course as a civilian conversion she was little more than an old airliner inside, but bobbing at her mooring off the giant slipway at White Cross Bay she was a tangible link back to a nearly forgotten part of the lake's history.

1   Smith, Peter, 1993. The Last Flying Boat, ML814 – Islander. Ensign Publications. 185455 083 7

2   Barnes, C H, 1967. Shorts Aircraft since 1900, Putnam.

At the northern end of White Cross Bay Islander turned again and began the take off run. At first she seemed to be travelling no faster than on the first run. It was only later that I found out one engine had not been developing full power but half way through the second take off run it suddenly burst into life. She lifted from the water leaving a trail of wake behind her and, holding low over the lake, continued south to Bowness Bay.

As Islander swung round the bay she rocked her wings in farewell and swept past Queen Adelaide's Hill, heading north for a final fly past over White Cross Bay. With the weak engine throttled back, she began a slow climb making height to get over Dunmail Raise. She was heading, appropriately, for Sunderland for a flypast at the town's air show before beginning the long trip south to Southampton.

She would not return to Windermere. In late 1992 she was bought by oil million-aire and vintage aircraft collector Kermit Weeks, who kept her airworthy at his Fantasy of Flight theme park in Florida.[3] Recently she has not flown and the chances of a return to the lake are remote.

And gradually, over time, the memories of Windermere's time as a centre of aircraft production fade once again.

Each year over 14 million tourists come to the Lake District but very, very few realise that it was a centre for aircraft production.

None come to look for disused aircraft factories and nobody seems to know that Windermere was the first place in the country to see an aircraft take off from water.

Rocking wings:
Islander sweeps past
Queen Adelaides Hill.

3   Smith, Peter, ibid

The beginnings

Visitors arriving in the Lake District today are presented with a consistent image. They will come in search of walking, Wordsworth, watersports, and then treat themselves to a decent meal afterwards. Few are aware of the industrial landscape they are spending their holidays in and rarely does industrial heritage feature on holiday plans.

It is not just the farming and forestry industries that have shaped the Lake District. There is hardly a hill that does not have a mine in it somewhere. The scree in the Langdales has been identified as a Stone Age axe factory and the timeshare nearby is on the site of a former gunpowder works.

But an aircraft factory?

Who in their right mind would put an aircraft factory in the Lake District? And who would decide it should build the most advanced aircraft of its time?

Yet that is exactly what did happen. The country watched mainland Europe fall before the might of a Nazi military machine and, with the nation's back to the wall, a far sighted strategy of expansion of aircraft production led to some creative solutions - but possibly none more so than the plan to move two massive buildings to Windermere for a new factory.

The two buildings were huge. The Detail Shop was 87,500 square feet in a conventionally designed building while the new Hangar was 75,000 feet in a radical cantilever design to give a single uninterrupted span. Adding in storage, the offices and canteen brought the total area up to 233,000 square feet. This compared to Short Brothers Seaplane Works in Rochester which had 550,000 square feet of floor space in 1943.

The Windermere works would be capable of employing 1,500 workers[1] making a major impact on the Lake District's workforce - as would the need to find accommodation for those workers.

Waterbird: The first aircraft to take off from water in the British Empire, flown by H Stanley Adams who is seen here at the controls.

John Gordon

---

1   "Wage Bill of Nearly £1,000,000. Facts and Figures of Lakeland's Sunderlands" Westmorland Gazette, 9 Feb 1946

And the product was the four engined Short Sunderland flying boat - itself massive, with a double-decker layout internally, measuring over 85 feet in length and with a 112 foot wingspan.[2]

But with so much inevitable criticism of the ability to build such a complex aircraft in the Lake District, why was Windermere chosen in the first place? The official reason was simply that it was a site with access to deep water.

But Windermere was also the birthplace of British maritime aviation. When few had even seen an aeroplane and every flight was newsworthy enough to be reported in the journals of the day, a small group of pioneers turned to Windermere as the testing ground for the first flight from water in Britain. Even Short Brothers' own chief test pilot, John Lankester-Parker, had worked as an instructor on float planes on the lake.[3]

In the early years of the 20th century, before the powerboat eclipsed the steam age on Windermere, more and more people had become involved in experiments with aircraft.

Although Orville Wright flew on 17th December 1903, flying did not really come to Britain until the first aviation meetings were held in October 1909.

At the now famous Blackpool meeting were two Westmorland men who were to become the leaders in the attempts to fly from water in Britain.

31-year-old Oscar Gnosspelius, a civil engineer who had worked in Sweden, South America and Africa, and Captain Edward William Wakefield, barrister, Westmorland County Councillor, estate manager and Lord of the Manor both resolved to take to the air themselves - and both decided to make use of Windermere.[4]

The reasoning was that the lake was freely available and a crash into the water should be more survivable than into a field. Against them were the difficulties of flying from water bearing in mind the poor performance of the engines of the day, mainly the added weight of the floats and the need to overcome the drag of the float being pulled across the lake surface, slowing the aircraft.

Gnosspelius started work designing his own aircraft and persuaded local boat builder Arthur Borwick to build it for him. First attempts to fly in August attracted large crowds of spectators. The aircraft could not do more than hop from the lake and was redesigned with a longer but lighter fuselage, while Gnosspelius enrolled in a flying school at Brooklands.

Meanwhile, Wakefield had built a hangar on his land at the Hill of Oaks and visited Henri Fabre at Marseilles, the first man to fly from water on 28th March 1910.[5]

Wakefield ordered an aircraft from the fledgling company A. V. Roe and when the American Glen Curtis flew from San Diego harbour on 26th January 1911,[6] Wakefield ordered a biplane of similar design. The aircraft flew on 19th June at Brooklands where Wakefield met the 27-year-old H. Stanley Adams, an engineer with Rolls Royce, who was offered the job as the test pilot at Windermere.

Both Wakefield and Gnosspelius became busy modifying their aircraft. Both fitted additional small hydroplane steps to the underside of the floats to pull air under the float and help it to break free from the lake's surface and by November 1911 both had machines capable of flight and were waiting for the right weather to make their attempts.

Saturday 25th November. After a week of bad weather, Gnosspelius taxied out onto the calm lake at Bowness Bay. The aircraft picked up speed, faster than before due to

2   Barnes, C H, 1967. Shorts Aircraft since 1900, Putnam.

3   Connon, Peter, 1984. An Aeronautical history of the Cumbria, Dumfries and Galloway Region. Part 2: 1915 to 1930, St Patrick's Press, 0 9508287 1 8.

4   Connon, Peter, 1982. In the Shadow of the Eagles Wing, The history of aviation in the Cumbria, Dumfries and Galloway Region 1825-1914, St Patrick's Press, 0 9508787 0 X.

5   King, H F, 1966. Aeromarine Origins, Putnam.

6   King, H F. ibid

Hill of Oaks: Short 827 Biplane 3328 flies past the hangar where FBA flying boat 3206 is on the slipway. The FBA has an earlier Union Flag on the tail showing through the weathered paint of the red white and blue stripes.

Peter Greetham

Lakes Pioneer: Oscar Gnosspelius taxying his Gnosspelius No. 2 on Windermere.

Peter Greetham

the latest modified float. Passing Belle Isle it left the water and, without warning, crabbed to the right. Unprepared, Gnosspelius, who had only learnt to fly straight and level at Brooklands, overcorrected and the port wing tip hit the water, flipping the machine onto its back. Gnosspelius was unhurt and clung to the aircraft until both he and it were rescued.

At the Hill of Oaks, Adams was unaware of the drama happening just to the north and made his attempt. The aircraft, known at the time only as the Avro Curtiss, failed to unstick on its first run up the lake but, with a light wind starting up from the north, Adams made another run.

After half a mile, it left the water and flew at 50 feet north along the lake.[7] The light wind had made all the difference and Adams became the first man in Britain to fly an aircraft from water. He made a wide turn at the ferry and returned to land at the Hill of Oaks. Several more flights were made that day and on Monday 27th November the aircraft, by then known as Waterbird, made two exhibition flights.

Sadly this remarkable flight is often overlooked when the history of "first flights" is recorded. The difficulty is that a commonly repeated mistake is given greater publicity and Wakefield's and Adams' achievements are not given the credit they are due.

One week before the calm day on Windermere, which brought out both Gnosspelius and Wakefield, a similar experiment was taking place at Barrow-in-Furness. Commander Oliver Schwann was attempting to fly from the Cavendish Dock at Barrow in an Avro D biplane, and employed a number of different experimental float designs. Eventually, and apparently to Schwann's surprise, he got airborne on 18th November 1911 reaching a height of 15 to 20 feet before losing control and crashing into the dock where the aircraft capsized.[8]

And this is where the trouble lies. To qualify as a first flight the aircraft is required to be under control. Both Schwann and Gnosspelius fail to take the title of first flight from water because they could not maintain control of their aircraft and crashed.

Later Waterhen:
Modifications saw
Waterhen operate with
twin main floats.
Sally Beckett

---

7   "Hydroaeroplanes on Lake Windermere" Flight, 9th December 1911.

8   A J Jackson, Avro Aircraft since 1908, 1965 (revised R T Jackson 1990) Putnam.

*Three men in a flying boat. H P Reid in the front
cockpit of FBA 3648 with DN Robertson and J L Parker behind.
The FBAs arrived at Windermere in early 1916.*

Sally Beckett

The Avro D did eventually fly successfully. In April 1912, piloted by S V Sippe, it made a number of flights from Barrow and became the first seaplane to successfully take off from British seawater.[9]

Those first flights and the setting up of the Lakes Flying Company a month later to teach flying and build aircraft did not go unnoticed locally, particularly when an application was made to build a hangar at Cockshot Point at Bowness.

The application brought a stream of protests about the flying on the lake - a pattern that has followed most of the aviation activities on Windermere over the years.

Champions of the protesters were children's author and farmer Beatrix Potter and Canon Hardwicke Rawnsley, founder of the National Trust. They argued that the aircraft had frightened horses being transported on the lake ferry and they posed a danger to a lake busy with pleasure boats.

On 5th January 1912 the Lake District Hydroaeroplane Protest Committee was set up and, in conjunction with the Lake District Defence Society, it launched a national campaign against the menace of the hydroaeroplanes. Over 10,000 signatures were gathered in a petition.

Wakefield fought back by pointing out the military benefits of aircraft, particularly hydroaeroplanes, for an island nation.

In one letter, with great foresight, he stated that "Scouting by hydroaeroplane will shortly become a necessity for the safety of this island."[10] Not only did he correctly predict the need for floatplanes in the Great War but also the role for the Sunderland flying boats that were to be built on the lake 30 years later.

*Flight training:
A group of students
waiting for instruction
on Waterhen.
L to R: C A Barber
(in Waterhen)
H A Benson, J A Coats,
H Shaw, W Laidler,
J L Parker, E R Yates,
D S C Macaskie,
A J S Inglis, P Ingham,
N K Lawton, and
H Robinson.*

Sally Beckett

9   A J Jackson, ibid

10 Connon, Peter, 1982. In the Shadow of the Eagles Wing, The history of aviation in the Cumbria, Dumfries and Galloway Region 1825-1914, St Patrick's Press, 0 9508787 0 X.

In April the government announced that they would not prohibit flying from the lake and the aviators were free to continue experimenting.

While this argument was going on Gnosspelius had repaired his damaged machine and on 14th February 1912 successfully flew it from Windermere.[11] He managed a series of flights during the day in the first successful aircraft built in Cumbria.

The Lakes Flying Company was also building a larger version of the Waterbird, which was lost when the Cockshot Point hangar collapsed in March 1912. The new aircraft, Waterhen, was large enough for a pilot and passenger and Wakefield briefly took flying lessons in it until a heavy landing damaged the floats and he gave up his flying career.

Passenger flights in Waterhen proved very popular and Wakefield brought other aircraft to the lake including another Avro Biplane to be named Seabird.

When war broke out in 1914 it was a serious blow to the Lakes Flying Company as Adams and Gnosspelius both signed up for service with the Royal Naval Air Service. Gnosspelius later left the RNAS to join Short Brothers and returned to the Lake District to live in Coniston in 1925. During World War Two he assisted Shorts with the local negotiations for their factory at White Cross Bay.[12]

William Roland Ding, brought to Windermere by Wakefield as an instructor, saw the possibilities for training pilots for the Admiralty Air Department. With his partners in the Northern Aircraft Company, he bought the Lakes Flying Company's three aircraft and a lease on the hangars.

The Northern Aircraft Company's school at Windermere was well under way when on 4th February 1915 Ding received a letter from John Lankester Parker,[13] an 18-year-old pilot who was turned down for war service because polio as a child had made him lame. He had learnt to fly at Vickers Flying School at Hendon and was to go on to be one of the most respected flying boat pilots. As chief test pilot for Short Brothers he returned

11   Connon, Peter, ibid

12   Connon, Peter, ibid

13   Connon, Peter, 1984. An Aeronautical history of the Cumbria, Dumfries and Galloway Region. Part 2: 1915 to 1930, St Patrick's Press, 0 9508287 1 8.

to the Lake District to test many of the Sunderlands built at the Windermere factory and was later a director of the company.

But in 1915 he was keen for work and offered to pay £10 for his conversion to flying hydroaeroplanes. His first flight from the lake was not an auspicious start to the great pilot's career at Windermere. Taking off in Waterhen with Ding he pulled back on the stick too early. The plane lurched into the air then fell back onto the lake with a resounding splash. Parker was described as "ham fisted" but in his defence said the elevators on Waterhen were grossly overbalanced. Despite the false start he was given the instructor's job.

Accidents to some of the original aircraft led to new machines being brought to Windermere, including two Blackburn aircraft. Closer links were established with the Admiralty when they delivered aircraft for use at the school and gave a contract to convert landplane pilots to fly hydroaeroplanes. Eventually, in May 1916, the Admiralty requisitioned the school with Parker, Ding and another instructor staying for a short time as civilian instructors. The school was named RNAS Hill of Oaks. [14] When Parker left he joined Short Brothers, and stayed with the company for over 30 years.

Several aircraft were brought to the hangars at the Hill of Oaks but not all flew. Among them were Nieuports and FBA flying boats built by the Franco British Aviation Company. After the last civilians left at the end of June 1916, the name was changed to RNAS Windermere.

Tragedy came to Windermere on 2nd September 1916 when 23 year-old F/Lt. H. A. Bower was killed flying an FBA.[15] He took off to demonstrate take off and landing techniques, unaware that the aircraft had been weakened by a previous heavy landing. As he approached to land the aircraft broke up in mid-air and fell into the lake. The pupil, Flight Sub Lieutenant. Thompson, was recovered suffering from shock and minor injuries but there was no trace of Bower, whose body was not recovered until five days later after dragging the lake. His was the first death in an aircraft accident in Cumbria.

By December 1916 the station had begun to be wound up with the last instructional flight recorded on 13th January 1917. By 27th February the last of the assorted aircraft had left the lake and RNAS Windermere was officially closed in June 1917.

It was over two years before aviation again returned to Windermere, this time with no apparent objections. A V Roe and Co set up pleasure flights across the north of England and on 21st July 1919 the winner of the 1914 Schneider Trophy race at Monte Carlo, Howard Cecil Pixton, arrived at Windermere in an AVRO 504K seaplane to run pleasure flights. His aircraft was joined by another AVRO 504K a week later

The Cockshot Point hangar was used to give passenger flights as well as charter flights to anywhere with deep water, and Pixton also started up a newspaper delivery service by taking the Daily News' Manchester edition to the Isle of Man.[16] The paper wanted the flights in order to have their papers on the island eight hours ahead of their rivals, which arrived by steamer. The first newspaper flight by Pixton for the AVRO Transport Company was on 4th August 1919. The special seaplane edition proved a big success and in subsequent flights all the copies were quickly snapped up. The publicity from the month-long experiment had benefited the newspaper and Pixton, who was in great demand for pleasure flights. In the third week of September he made 32 flights from Windermere. However, the business was only short-lived.

Pixton's flights from Windermere in late 1919 proved to be the last for some time. Windermere reverted to its traditional boating activities and, apart from an occasional flying visitor, aviation did not return until the war made it necessary for Windermere to once more be home to its own aircraft industry.

14   Connon, Peter, ibid

15   Connon, Peter, ibid

16   "Douglas-Windermere Flights", Flight, 14 August 1919.

The battle to build

A trip to Cockshot Point today or even to the Hill of Oaks will result in the discovery of nothing to indicate that aircraft ever flew from Windermere. It is hard to even imagine an aircraft hangar on Cockshot Point today. But in the early days of World War II, memories of those early days of pioneering flights from Windermere would still have been fresh when a country at war again was looking for suitable sites in which to build flying boats.

In 1940 the Government drew up plans to build a secret aircraft factory at Windermere.[1] The need for the factory was clear. At the outbreak of war there were four squadrons equipped with Sunderlands - just 38 aircraft.[2] The number was rapidly increased and production was stepped up, reaching a peak in 1943 when 202 aircraft were built.[3] Initially the Sunderland was produced at Short Brothers' main factory at Rochester but additional production lines were added first at Blackburn's aircraft factory at Dumbarton and then later at Short and Harland in Belfast.

The Ministry of Aircraft Production (MAP) wanted to expand production at Rochester and plans were also under way to build two massive new sheds. The steelwork had been bought and foundations laid when it was decided the buildings should be built elsewhere because of the risk of bombing. An urgent search for sites centred on Windermere. Detailed reports on the feasibility of the dispersal were in MAP hands by November 1940.[4] The factory was not to be a shadow factory but was always considered a dispersal of buildings and production from Rochester.

The Ministry expected production to be two aircraft per month, along with the new prototype flying boat, the Shetland, which was being designed to replace the Sunderland. Initially it was thought that up to 1,200 workers would transfer from Rochester to the Lake District with a further 300 or so employed locally. It turned out that workers had to be brought in from many parts of the country.

The hangar would be the largest single span building in the country, some said the world, at 75,000 square feet. More conventionally built, the machine shop would be even larger at 87,500 square feet together with nearly another 50,000 square feet for offices, canteen and stores. Despite the size of the factory, the machine shop was planned to be built in just 12 weeks and the hangar, offices and final fitting out was expected to take only 25 weeks from the date the project was given the go ahead.

Against the scheme was the sheer cost of the dispersal. An initial estimate showed that over £226,000 was needed when only

Old Friends: Windermere pioneer Oscar Gnosspelius and Short Brothers test pilot John Lankester Parker worked together in the 1920s when Gnosspelius tried some radical ideas in his Gnosspelius Gull. They are seen here with the aircraft – and a dog.

Sally Beckett

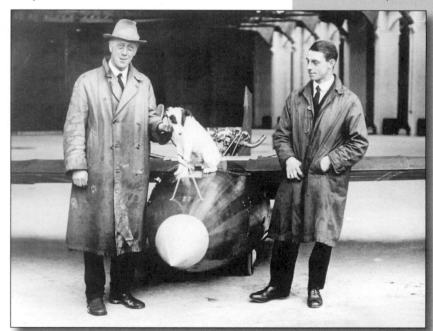

1   Short Brothers Rochester and Bedford Ltd, local objections to the factory premises, Windermere. AVIA 15/3622 The National Archives.

2   Delve, Ken, 1994. The source book of the RAF, Airlife 1 85310 451 5

3   Bowyer, Chaz, 1989. The Short Sunderland, Aston publications. 0 7110 0665 2

4   Short Brothers Rochester and Bedford Ltd, local objections to the factory premises, Windermere. AVIA 15/3622 The National Archives.

Short Brothers (Rochester & Bedford) Ltd.
Aeronautical Engineers.

Seaplane Works.
Rochester, Kent.

PLEASE ADDRESS YOUR
REPLY TO THE FIRM
AND QUOTE REFERENCE   AG/WLC/7

17th December, 1940.

Col. J.J. Llewellin,
Parliamentary Secretary to the Ministry of Aircraft Production,
Millbank,
LONDON S.W.I.

Dear Colonel Llewellin,

    Further to the discussion I had with you and the Supply Committee yesterday concerning the "Sunderland" dispersal scheme to Windermere, it was reported to me on my return to Rochester in the evening that a stick of bombs had been dropped on the other side of the river, which is about a quarter of a mile away from this factory.

    I feel, therefore, that we should treat this dispersal scheme as urgent and arrive at a decision as soon as possible.

    I can assure you I have given the matter considerable thought and I do not know of a better suggestion to put up than that already proposed, and as I stated to the Supply Committee we would be wise to try and anticipate and do this part of "Sunderland" dispersal in an orderly fashion.

        Yours sincerely,

Dispersal demand: Arthur Gouge, wrote to the Ministry of Aircraft Production to call for urgency in the Sunderland production dispersal, not knowing that the decision had been taken the day before.

£128,000 was in hand in Government budgets for the extension to the Seaplane Works at Rochester.[5] But added to that had to be the cost of the canteen, Air Raid Precautions equipment, tools and fittings for the factory which could not be transferred from Rochester. These totalled at least another £100,000 plus unspecified costs of the land at White Cross Bay and transporting all the materials, equipment and manpower from Rochester to Windermere.

But then the whole project hit a snag.

In Westmorland the concern was not about the costs but simply to the idea of building an aircraft factory in the Lake District at all. The fact that there was a war on didn't diminish the objections – it only prevented the arguments from being played out in local newspapers as had happened almost 30 years before.

The very thing that made the Lake District safe for dispersal of production – its distance from the German bombers – also meant it was chosen as a safe area for refugees. One of the first opponents was the Westmorland County Council, who suggested Coniston would be better, arguing that Windermere was already overcrowded with refugees. A letter received from Isobel McGregor-Rose stated that the government "proposes to turn [Windermere] into a place with a military objective. It seems to me to be the height of folly. Soon, at this rate of spoilation, there will be no safe spot left not to mention beauty spots."[6]

Another complication was the position of the factory close to the Ethel Headley Hospital - the hangar would be just 300 yards from it. The hospital at Calgarth housed

Stirling lines hit: The production of the Short Stirling was interrupted when the factory at Rochester Airport was hit by German bombers.

Sally Beckett

Rochester blitz: The gatehouse at the Seaplane Works was hit by a mine in April 1941 causing a loss of 63,000 sq. ft. of offices and production space.

Sally Beckett

5   Short Brothers Rochester and Bedford Ltd, local objections to the factory premises, Windermere. AVIA 15/3622 The National Archives.

6   McGregor Rose, Isobel, undated letter to MAP in AVIA 15 3622. The National Archives.

Hangar Foundations: Work starts on the lakeshore site where the hangar is to be built.

via Derek Hurst

Factory Foundations: The thick concrete raft which formed the foundations was being laid in April 1941.

88307-2 Bombardier via Ron Parsons

Slipway Construction: Even working at shallow depths in the early 1940s needed a full brass helmeted diving suit.

via Derek Hurst

40 children and was owned by Mr. O. W. E. Headley who also owned the land at White Cross Bay.

Hard on the heels of these objections, the Parliamentary Secretary to the Minister, Col. J. J. Llewellin, received a deputation that represented the Conservative private members committee, the National Trust and Friends of the Lake District. The Secretary of State for War, the local Conservative MP Oliver Stanley, was another opponent of the scheme.

They stated bluntly that they did not want the factory to be built at Windermere. However, if the project had to go ahead they said that it should be removed after the war, hotels should be requisitioned rather than building houses for the workers and trees on the lakeshore should be protected.

All of this debate generated considerable paperwork circulated round the Ministry in a manila folder. It is fortunate indeed that this one file was selected for preservation at the National Archives.[7] Flicking through the papers, chronologically ordered with the most recent on top and supporting documents filed alongside, it is possible to feel the sheer bewilderment among the mandarins in their Whitehall offices. Surely, they must have asked, don't the people in Windermere know there is a war on?

The internal discussions at the MAP revealed that their concerns with the scheme had gone further than the initial cost and local opposition. Ministers were worried about the shortage of labour in the north west of England in 1940. There were too many factories for the available workforce and, with few skilled workers in the Windermere area, there were some who felt the Windermere scheme should be rejected on labour grounds alone.

Alternative locations where there was labour, such as Dundee, were suggested, as was Belfast Lough to expand

7   Short Brothers Rochester and Bedford Ltd, local objections to the factory premises, Windermere. AVIA 15/3622 The National Archives.

production at Short and Harland. The difficulties of taking parts across the Irish Channel were the main disadvantages for the Belfast option.

Then, very late in the day, the Ministry was persuaded to look at the old seaplane works at Lytham St. Annes as a possible site. A hurried assessment was made which found that although there had been two seaplane sheds totalling 30,000 square feet, one had been pulled down and the other was being used by a bakery. Of the 20 feet wide slipway only 150 feet was clear with the rest under sand and mud. A brief appraisal noted that there was only about two or three hours floatation at the slipway and concluded, "The whole area is a dangerous mudflat and the site is altogether so unpromising that S/Ldr. Freeman does not propose to write a report on it unless requested." [8]

As the files grew ever thicker and more ideas were explored, the worst scenario was developing: the whole project was being delayed at a time when speed was of the greatest urgency.

By December Short Brothers' director and chief designer Arthur Gouge was becoming concerned at the delays and called on the Government to hurry their decision. He pointed out that German bombs had missed the Rochester factory by just quarter of a mile and added that he "did not know of a better suggestion than that already proposed."[9]

However, when he wrote the letter he was not to know that just the day before on 16th December 1940 the Ministry's Supply Board had taken the decision to go ahead with building the factory at Windermere.

The decision to build at Windermere included some compromises and Col. Llewellin set about mollifying the objectors with his letter which stated, "One of Shorts factories at Rochester has already been bombed. It would be madness now to erect further buildings there. Another site has to be found. The product is a flying boat. A site on the edge of deep water is essential. We have, therefore, had to decide on Windermere. I am sorry. Time, however, is all important."

Keel Jigs: With the hangar shell completed, the fitting out of the interior begins. In the foreground are the fuselage jigs - the spikes bolted to the floor will support the keel from which the whole fuselage is built.

88307-21
Bombardier
via Ron Parsons

---

8   Supply Board memo to MAP. 6-12-1940 in AVIA 15/3622, The National Archives
9   Arthur Gouge, letter to MAP. 17-12-1940 in AVIA 15/3622, The National Archives

More importantly for all the objectors, they were given an assurance from Col. Llewellin on behalf of the Minister that the factory would be removed from the site as soon after the war as practical.

"I have Lord Beaverbrook's authority to say that we undertake to have these buildings taken down as soon as the military situation makes it safe to do so at the end of the war. A slipway will be constructed and my undertaking does not extend to taking that up," Llewellin said.

Although Llewellin's undertakings stopped the objections to the factory it was only for a short time. After the war a campaign was mounted to keep the much needed industry and its jobs in the Lake District, but the Friends of the Lake District would not let the Government forget their undertakings to have all the buildings removed, a promise which was eventually kept.

The assurances did not, however, prevent a far lengthier debate about whether or not houses should be built for the workforce. Those who feared the Lake District's charms would be spoilt by heavy industry moving in were even more vocal when it came to building an entire village to house the workers for the new factory.

The debate over housing rumbled on in the background as urgent priority was given to starting work on the construction at White Cross Bay.

Hangar Framework: Seen from the slipway, the unusual cantilever framework for the hangar is almost finished.
88307-5 Bombardier via Ron Parsons

It would appear that the initial timetable for the construction was not met. It was not too surprising considering the problems that the contractors had to deal with on site.

The land at White Cross Bay was known to be prone to flooding and was described by locals as "just a big bog". The marsh was filled in with tons of rock waste brought across from the slate quarries in Langdale and at Coniston. On top of the slate waste was then poured the concrete foundations for the buildings and roadways. The roads and smaller buildings had three to four feet of concrete but the hangar itself had a base between eight and nine feet thick. More than sixty years after they were laid the foundations were still there, providing the White Cross Bay caravan site with a solid base for newly built chalets.

Photographs of the factory being built were helpfully dated and show that the first priority was the detail shop, where small parts and sub assemblies were manufactured. The first parts needed in the construction of the flying boats could then be started while the hangar was still being built.

Weatherproof: The size
of the Detail Shop can
be seen from the scale
of the workers fitting
the roof.
via Derek Hurst

In fact the detail shop was finished and fitted out by July 1941 [see photo below] with office staff housed temporarily while their own building was built nearby.

The day the canteen was finished and food became available was well remembered by the staff and workers. The kitchens had not accustomed themselves to coping with the large demand for food and one worker recalled that on the first day lunch did not end until well after 3pm. However, things soon settled down to a more regular pattern.

By the time the detail shop was complete, most of the steelwork for the hangar was erected by the lakeshore. The building was more complex than anything else in the region, involving a cantilever structure to support the roof which also carried four ten ton

Production Starts:
The interior
of the Detail Shop was
complete by July 1941
allowing training and
production to start.
*88307-4 Bombardier
via Ron Parsonss*

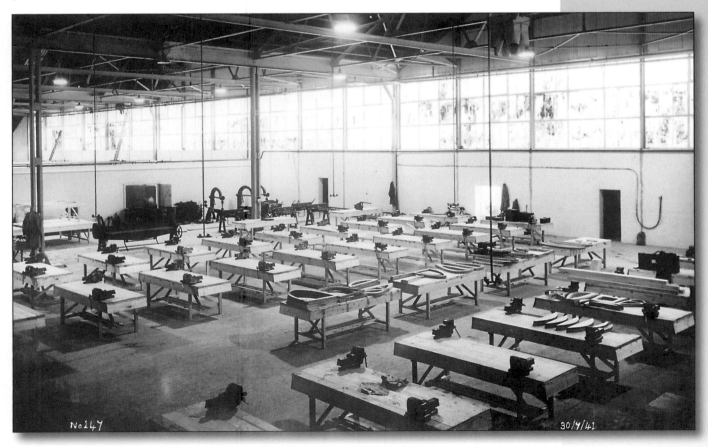

cranes used for lifting parts of the aircraft. One factory worker, Jim Dunlop, had worked as a plumber on the construction and remembered the warning given by the foreman when the cranes were first used.

"He told us that there would be a huge rattle but not to be worried because the building would never move again. Well there was this noise like thousands of plates being dropped all at once but he was right, it never did move again after that."

The hangar was 40 feet to the top of the doors and 70 feet to the roof tops and measured 300 feet by 250 feet. It was built on the lakeshore some distance from the detail shop, with a channel dug between the two to link all the necessary services of heating, water and electricity.

The ministry had to spend an additional £30,000 for Air Raid Precautions (ARP), including £7,000 for shelters alongside every building, blast walls, wire netting in the roofs and "dufaynet" covering to prevent windows shattering. Close to each building was a fire station, money was spent on black out, and camouflage paint for the building completed the scheme. But the greatest protection for the factory was its very remoteness. The only real scare was when some bombs were dropped on open country near Troutbeck and it was feared a raid had targeted the factory. It was quickly realised that the bombs had come from one aircraft jettisoning its load, probably unable to complete a trip to the dockyards in Barrow

The Air Raid shelters did get some use, being popular with courting couples and equally popular with the young boys who ran down the corridor linking them shining torches into the shelters, to the annoyance of the courting couples.

White Cross Bay in 1940 had no facilities for boats and two small jetties and a large slipway had to be built. The jetties, built up with cement bags, were used for the pinnace and tenders which ferried crews to and from aircraft on the lake while the slipway had to be large enough to cope with the Sunderlands. It was built 100 yards out into the lake by divers wearing the heavy brass air fed helmets that preceded modern wet suits.

The hangar was finally completed by March 1942 in time to accept the first flying boat hulls which had been laid in the detail shop.

Within another two months the entire complex of buildings, roads and services had been finished and, more importantly, the first Sunderlands were already well on their way to completion.

The urging of the MP's delegation to preserve trees on the site had clearly been heeded. Indeed much additional planting was carried out, largely to help with the camouflaging of the factory. Passers by on the road from Windermere to Ambleside might not have realised the extent of the factory behind the trees which was starting its contribution to the nation's defence. Beyond the gates the neatly laid out roads and pathways were lined with newly planted shrubberies. The first workers looked proudly round their own "garden factory", often taking their lunch on the small hill overlooking the site or down by the lake.

For many it would have been easy to forget that there was a war going on.

Recruiting

On 18th September 1940 14 year old Peter Greetham and his family were bombed out of their house at Rochester. The family had been in a dug-out when the bomb landed and, although their home was destroyed, they were uninjured.

Peter had succeeded in being awarded an apprenticeship with Shorts where his father, George, was working on the plans for the Windermere factory. Arriving back one night at the street where they had been forced to move he found the road blocked by debris following another bombing raid. Relieved to find the family had again survived George Greetham announced that they were all moving to Windermere, as soon as possible.

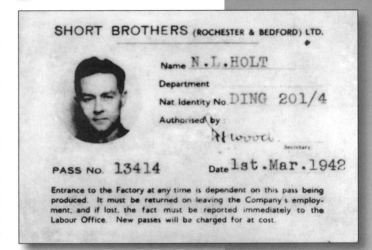

Factory Pass: Nick Holt was one of the inspectors who moved to Windermere from Rochester.

Nick and Rita Holt

George Greetham was appointed manager of the new factory and on 14th August 1941 his son Peter became one of very few apprentices at the Windermere works, earning 13/9 a week. His birthday brought a raise to 14/- a week. Knowing that the factory would have to close after the war Shorts would not take on local boys as apprentices, but the few who followed their parents from the Medway to White Cross Bay were allowed to transfer their training.

Building the factory was one thing but finding the necessary skilled workforce proved to be quite a different problem. As Britain's industrial might was directed to military uses, skilled workers were in short supply. Workers were told they were in reserved occupations and prevented from being called up so the Government could direct them to where they were needed most.

The main industries in the Lake District, farming, mining and boat building, were never likely to produce the large workforce needed to man the new flying boat factory, never mind providing skilled workers. However, the Sunderland designer Arthur Gouge, himself a carpenter, believed boat builders made good aircraft builders and planned to employ some skilled men from the local boat yards.[1] It was planned to recruit 300 men locally and to bring the other 1200 needed from Rochester. But Short Brothers had enough trouble in Rochester keeping up with production of the Sunderland at the Seaplane Works and the Stirling bomber at Rochester Airport without sending so many workers north.

The shortage of manpower was a nationwide problem and salvation came in December 1941 with the Government's decision to introduce conscription for women. The choice was to join the women's sections of the armed forces or to do war work, in the fields with the land army or in the factories. Across the land women took on jobs in heavy industry, tackling welding and riveting with dexterity. Windermere was no different.

The total number working for Shorts in Windermere peaked at 1,571 in 1942[2] but of this an amazing 47 per cent were "diluted" labour, the young boys not yet old enough to be called up and women brought in to fill essential roles. The core of foremen and senior staff came from Rochester as expected but in nothing like the numbers the ministry had wanted. Many others had to be drafted in from other aircraft firms and even Austins in Birmingham, whose car production lines has been converted to help with the war effort.

---

1   Short Brothers Rochester and Bedford Ltd, local objections to the factory premises, Windermere. The National Archives AVIA 15/3622

2   Wage Bill of Nearly £1,000,000. Facts and Figures of Lakeland's Sunderlands. 9 Feb 1946, Westmorland Gazette.

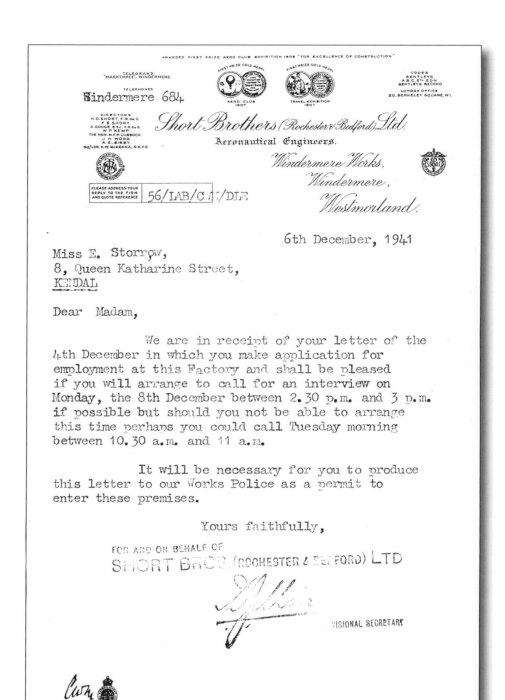

In Rochester Nick Holt had served his apprenticeship at Shorts as a fitter and had moved up to work as an inspector before being asked to go to Windermere. His wife, Rita and father-in-law Alf Peckham were also Shorts workers and endured the regular air raids on the Medway towns before they were sent north to Windermere. Every night was spent sleeping in the shelters and work was disrupted by the German bombers. The tracing office where Mrs. Holt worked was evacuated to the far side of the Medway river to be further from the raids. The seaplane works was found to be vulnerable when a mine hit the works in April 1941[3] causing serious damage to the main office block and other buildings near to the gatehouse. Fortunately the flying boat production lines were undamaged.

The gaps in skilled workers were mostly filled with already trained staff from other factories, some of whom showed a reluctance to travel to Windermere. Norman Parker worked for Fairey Aviation at Heaton Chapel near Manchester, building the Fairey Battle

---

3   Reconstruction Scheme for North End of Seaplane Works, Rochester, March 1942, Short Brothers, Rochester and Bedford Ltd.

bomber, when he was ordered to move to another factory. He found himself standing with others in a queue for shipbuilding at Barrow while alongside another queue of men was going to Shorts at Windermere. Next to him a colleague berated his transfer to Windermere.

"Windermere! Out in the bloody wilderness," he said. Mr. Parker took the chance and swapped places, delighted to be going to the Lake District. He arrived at Windermere railway station expecting to meet the 12 others from Faireys when he arrived, but found he was alone. It was a Saturday and he made his way down to the works to report for duty. By the time his workmates finally turned up on the Wednesday he had already been promoted to chargehand.

Another worker delighted to find himself transferred to Windermere was Jim Frearson, originally a cabinet maker from Kendal. When he had tried to join the Fleet Air Arm he was told he was in a reserved occupation and sent to work for A. V. Roe in Manchester, initially working on the Anson trainer and then as a flying control engineer on the Avro Manchester bomber and later its successor the famous Avro Lancaster.

One day he was called to an interview at a hotel and recalls being told sternly that he had been transferred. He was asked: "You have been transferred to Windermere - have you heard of it?" Repressing a grin, he said he had and was soon in charge of fitting flying controls and automatic pilot systems to all the Sunderlands to come out of the Windermere works.

By a variety of means Shorts gathered at Windermere most of the skilled staff they needed. There were still gaps, and one local girl found herself given a large book on electroplating which was the closest she came to formal training.

There were many local girls who wanted to join Shorts to "do their bit" for the war effort. Many shops in Kendal, Windermere and Ambleside found their staff, short of work because of rationing, deserting to build flying boats. They could not and did not object to the loss, such was the feeling

Gatehouse: The entrance to the factory had, on the right, the gatehouse, home guard hut and armoury. The hangar can be seen beyond.   **88307-10 Bombardier via Ron Parsons**

Air Raid Shelters: Simple brick-built structures, the air raid shelters around the Detail Shop never had to be used.   ***via Derek Hurst***

Neatly Laid Out: The bridge and the paths of the factory here still survive today. This railing today shows it was probably painted green and white - to aid visibility in blackouts.   ***via Derek Hurst***

that the whole country had to work together in the dark days of the early war years.

The first workers at Windermere only had one building to occupy. The massive detail shop, by the main road, was the first to be completed so that work could start on the huge number of parts needed to build a Sunderland while the hangar was still be built.

The first task was to get production started. The production sequence was already tried and tested at Rochester, but with so many staff with more enthusiasm than skill, on the job training was to be an important feature for some time to come. Some fitters were sent to Kendal on a six week training course, others went to Preston or further afield, but for many their training was all done in the factory.

Completed hangar:
With the jetty and
fuel pumps ready,
the hangar was
finished by June 1942
via Derek Hurst

Senior chargehand Llew Llewellyn recalled how it was decided to train workers to make what was needed for the next two weeks only. Once the job had been mastered and that stage of work completed the workers were shown the next stage of the construction - a procedure which would continue until the first aircraft flew.

Many of the new employees found themselves working on the benches, armed with patterns and jigs to guide their first attempt at aircraft construction. Each job had to be completed in a particular time that was set in a complicated process by the rate fixers. Taking too long would mean a docking of pay but completing the job early could bring bonuses.

Not all the young boys new to the factory appreciated how the system worked. Stan Fearon was caught out on just his second task at the benches.

Windermere Lodgings:
Calgarth could
not accommodate
all the workers
in the factory and
this group, part
of the contingent
from Birmingham,
were among
many in lodgings
in Windermere.
Norman Parker

"I was given triangular shaped blocks of aluminium to file down to a particular shape. I stood at the bench and filed away with great enthusiasm. I could see people laughing as I worked but I kept going with the sweat pouring off me. When I finished them I found I had done the job in a third of the time allowed. The chargehands, the rate fixers and the unions were all called in to sort it out. They weren't going to pay me treble time for it. Eventually it was agreed that I could have double time for it but it killed the time on that job for anybody else doing it - they all had to do it much faster from then on!"

Similar problems occurred as new machinery was brought in. Because the factory was started in a hurry, a lot of jobs were done by hand until the necessary machines, all in short supply because of the demands of the war effort, were in place.

One young worker benefited when set to work in the machine shop with brand new equipment for putting screw threads onto particular items. Left to himself he worked away until four days later he had a huge pile of the tiny parts alongside him. The rate fixers had been caught out by the efficiency of the new machine and that week he went home with a bulging pay packet.

Of course the bonuses could only be paid if the parts were good enough to be used. In those first few months of learning

the job, many were nowhere near the right standard. Parts made for aircraft had to be to a high level of accuracy and there was a double system for checking.

The government Aeronautical Inspection Directorate (AID) inspectors were ultimately responsible for ensuring that the aircraft were fit for duty with the RAF. They had to oversee the work being done by Short Brothers' own inspectors who ensured work was up to standard and also authorised payment. Because they were on piece work, the workers would have strong views of the inspectors depending on whether their work was accepted or not.

In the early days of the training there were major problems with the quality of work and for the first weeks everything went into the scrap bin. Inspector Nick Holt was on the receiving end more than once.

"For the first few months standards were shocking. Many of the bits made went straight in the bin. I got threatened one day because I turned a girl's work down and she had not got paid. The first 12 months were rough"

Gradually experience was gained and the workforce settled to their task. A pattern of work was created which soon had the whole factory working to the tight schedule needed to get the Sunderlands to the RAF on time.

Top photo: Offices: Looking along the footpath between the Detail Shop on the right and the offices on the left, can be seen the chimneys of the boiler house. **Derek Hurst**

Middle photo: Work Starts: This view shows work underway in the Detail Shop by November 1941. A few parts are visible on the benches with engine nacelles beyond and, in the distance, the first fuselages in the temporary jigs that were later moved to the hangar. **Peter Greetham**

Bottom photo: Growing camouflage: Planting around the office block and elsewhere gave the site a pleasant garden factory appearance, although planting had been paid for as part of the camouflage for the Air Raid Precautions **Derek Hurst**

Production starts

From the road passing White Cross Bay today it is hard to see the scale of the former factory site through the trees. It would have been much the same when the factory was built, with the trees preserved to aid the camouflaging. The hangar by the lake and associated works would all have been out of sight from passers-by while only the back wall of the detail shop would have loomed up behind the trees.

The detail shop was the largest building on the site at 87,500 square feet. It housed the departments concerned with the major manufacturing of the factory capable of producing most of the items needed in building the flying boats.

In the centre of the building small rooms were home to the electroplating and anodic treatment sections. Much of the rest of the building was given over to the cutting shop, machine shop and a press shop. Much heavy machinery was in use but, with automation not yet a common sight, there were also many benches where parts were shaped and worked by hand.

When the building opened in mid 1941, none of the other buildings on the site were ready. The production office was set up in a mezzanine floor along one side of the building and controlled the supply of raw materials into the works.

While the staff settled in to learning their new job, their permanent home was under construction just outside. Eventually the blueprint library would occupy the mezzanine floor.

To see the procedures used it is perhaps best to follow the production sequence through the various departments of the factory.

The whole process was controlled through the production office, housed in the single storey building outside the detail shop. The offices included those of Francis Short,

Machine Room: The lathes and other machinery were largely imported from the USA under the lend-lease deal. There is not yet much machinery - more arrived later as production got fully underway.

Peter Greetham

son of Horace Short, one of the original three Short Brothers, and George Greetham, the factory manager.

Harold Trennah was in charge of the production office and, with his core of trained Rochester staff, the local workers were guided through the operation of the system brought in from the Seaplane works. The system had been studied and written up in Aircraft Engineering Magazine in 1939 when they were invited to see the building of flying boats at Rochester.[1]

The system started in the Drawing Office, which created a list of materials needed. This materials schedule was sent to the Production Office where the materials requisition chits were made out. These were passed to the Rate Fixers who were responsible for working out which tools and jigs would be needed in consultation with foremen. An order would then be created for the Jig and Tool Drawing Office.

Cutting Room:
The guillotine
in the foreground was
used for cutting sheets
of aluminium alloy
while a bandsaw and
other machinery can
also be seen.
Peter Greetham

Once all the parts needed had been worked through this system it was possible to calculate how long it would take to make each component and the order they were needed on the production line. Progress charts were created showing exactly when worked needed to start on each part or component so the construction of an aircraft wouldn't be held up for want of a small part.

The first stage would be the manufacture of frames and the keel sections while the last two stages were fitting of wing tip floats and the flying controls.

The first parts of this production system had already been fine tuned at Rochester and all the timings already worked out. So the production office was in charge of making sure raw materials were ordered in time, and instructions on which parts were needed were passed down to the shop floor at the right time.

In addition to the sheets of steel or aircraft grade aluminium - Dural - there were countless other items needed ranging from forgings, castings and extrusions to electrical equipment and even engines, which all had to be ordered. All of them had to be listed onto cards by the production office as they arrived. As they were used up on the shop floor, they were deleted from the cards giving the office a constant check on what was in stock and what needed ordering. Running efficiently everything would be available when needed, but with the war on delays were often beyond the control of Short's staff, even though the government set up offices to smooth out delays in deliveries between factories.

Parts came from Rochester but also a wide variety of sources across the country. Mrs. Ada Burrow remembered how even just the de-icing equipment for the aircraft consisted of more than 100 different parts - each had to be ordered separately.

"We didn't even know what they all were, we were just expected to go in and get on with the job," she said.

Alongside the production office was the drawing office which employed three draughtsmen and two tracers. The draughtsmen produced the production drawings in pencil, which were copied by the tracers onto linen. The linen was treated to make it transparent and from this master a number of blueprints could be made. Occasionally alterations were made to the production of the aircraft and in each case a new drawing was needed. Shorts worked in conjunction with the Ministry of Aircraft Production who ordered changes

1 Flying Boat Construction. August, 1939, Aircraft Engineering.

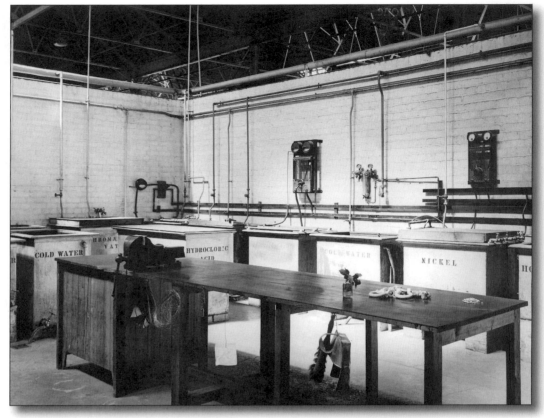

as problems showed up in operation of the aircraft. The appropriate drawings had to be found, altered and changes passed down to the factory floor. One of the special jobs for the office was to produce a map of the lake with the heights of nearby hills all marked to help visiting pilots. The drawings were all stored in the blueprint library on the mezzanine floor of the detail shop where they would be readily available.

Librarian Majorie Crosland recalled the system for issuing the blueprints.

"There was a department attached to the library run by a Mrs. Davies where the drawings were mounted onto cardboard and laminated to stop them getting oily and damaged. People who had a drawing were supposed to bring them back. We had people continuously issuing and receiving documents and filing them away."

The drawings were in five scales, with the most detailed showing the individual parts while the larger scales showed complete assemblies.

Sharing the office, alongside the production staff, were the rate fixers who set a time for each job on the factory floor. Knowing what work was needed and the times they would take, schedules for the production process were drawn up and passed out.

The procedures in the office were, by their nature, complicated, but once running smoothly they ensured the maximum efficiency from the shop floor and kept the finished products, completed aircraft, rolling out of the hangar at the required rate of two a month.

The office prepared job sheets for each part to be made and the necessary raw materials were collected from the stores. Most of the parts were hand made and would pass through the hands of several workers before being finally fitted to the airframe.

For instance, to make the ribs for the fuselage, sheets of Dural were cut on the massive powered guillotines in the cutting shop. Passed to the machine shop they were then folded on presses to the correct pattern before being passed on again. They were made in roughly the correct lengths but still had to be cut and fitted to the airframe. Once fitted

correctly they were given corrosion protection and only then would the riveters be able to fix them permanently in place. For a more complex area, parts could pass through far greater numbers of hands.

In 1940 there was a shortage of machinery because of the rapid expansion, not just in aircraft factories but all industries manufacturing for the war effort. As the Windermere works was brought into operation more and more mechanisation was brought into the machine shop. Massive Cincinnati milling machines and other equipment were brought over from America on the very same Atlantic convoys which the Sunderlands were later to protect from the U-Boat wolf packs. The machinery came

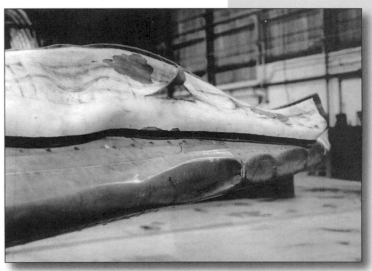

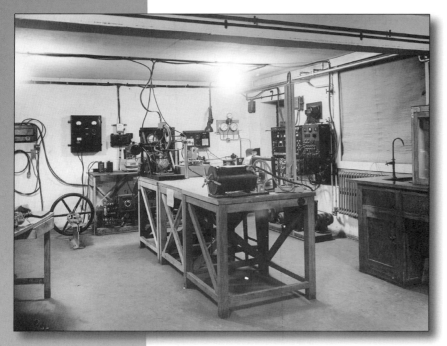

Testing, Testing:
The testing workshop
in the Detail Shop,
with a wide range
of equipment for
electrical, chemical
and physical tests.
Peter Greetham

to the UK under the lend lease deal which brought aircraft and tanks from the USA to supply UK forces.

Workers in the machine shop were often moved from job to job. One day it could be making bolts, another milling slots in some component before back to the lathes turning items.

The largest piece of machinery in the machine shop was also perhaps the most surprising to find at Windermere. Photographs show that Shorts installed a wing spar milling machine at Windermere despite the fact that wings were never made in the Lake District.

Some senior workers from the factory deny that the milling machine ever produced spars at the factory, but there was a logic to its being there, even if unused. In Rochester number one shop produced wing spars and built up the complete wings for the Sunderlands. The wings were loaded onto transporters and driven the long, and in the 1940s, twisty journey north - occasionally causing some damage to the wing tips which overhung the rear of the trailer by some distance.

The wings from Rochester were made to a high standard, assembled in a sophisticated jig to ensure that every one was exactly the same. The RAF insisted on an interchangeability standard so that a wing from one aircraft could be used to replace a damaged wing on another. Previously with the civil aircraft such as the C-Class flying boats, although the wings were built accurately, they were assembled in simple jigs with the use of old fashioned spirit levels and plumb bobs, effectively hand built. The military methods were those of mass production.

But with the threat to Rochester from German bombers, if the wing production had been seriously damaged, how could production have continued at Windermere? The wing spar milling machine was no ordinary piece of equipment. It was highly specialised, but by taking the trouble of installing it at Windermere Short Brothers were buying an insurance against damage in Rochester.

The wing spars on the Sunderland were actually an oblong box structure built up from four T-shaped sections braced with tubular struts. The T sections were formed from L40 alloy extruded bars of up to 22 feet.[2] Finding a way to machine the sections to make the spars initially caused a problem since the tolerance had to be within 0.005 inch - and the spars tapered in all three dimensions. With no machine able to mill the sections to such close tolerances, the Short Brothers engineers built their own. It was one of these machines that was installed at Windermere.

It is also clear from photos that engine nacelles were manufactured at Windermere. These were also not needed, as the wings arrived on the low loaders with the nacelles already fitted.

It seems likely that the empty trailers were loaded up with spars and engine nacelles and possibly other equipment for the journey back to Rochester. This was efficient use of the dispersal scheme. There was no point in having empty lorries moving about the country and supplying parts to the other factories was the most sensible use of any additional capacity at Windermere.

---

2   Flying Boat Construction. August, 1939, Aircraft Engineering.

It is not recorded where Windermere supplied parts were sent but, of course, there were other factories at both Dumbarton and Belfast producing Sunderlands.

The engine nacelles were a good example of the work in the subassembly section in the detail shop. The benches and machine shop produced the basic parts from raw materials and passed them on to the next section. Here the sub assemblies would be built up, using the larger scale drawings. Typical subassemblies would be the nacelles mounted onto the wings, doors and hatches and even the tail section of the fuselage that was built on steel girder jigs in the detail shop.

With the hangar not yet finished, the first keels were laid in the detail shop and six fuselages were started before the jigs were moved down to the hangar. However, the tail section assembly, under the guidance of chargehand Jock Large, was always built in the detail shop, using pretty much the same techniques as for the main fuselage itself. The frames were first suspended

Below: Detail Shop. The main work area shows the essentially handbuilt nature of the aircraft. From the roof hangs a propaganda poster showing an RAF fighter swooping over a downed German aircraft. The poster reads "The RAF are doing a fine job, This plant will help them finish it." (See detail at right)
Peter Greetham

THE *RAF* ARE DOING A FINE JOB

-this plant will help them to finish it!

Peter Greetham

from the jigs and then stringers linked them to form a metal skeleton before the plates were riveted to hold the whole thing together. Built on small trolleys, they were able to be towed down to the hangar to be mated up to the fuselage sections.

In the centre of the detail shop were some closed off rooms, almost perpetually wreathed in steam with the pungent aromas of acids and solvents drifting across the rest of the work floor. These were the rooms which housed the electroplating, annealing and anodising departments. All the aluminium parts of the aircraft had to be both annealed and anodised.

The annealing process involved heating and slow cooling to strengthen the metal. Once cut, drilled and bent the sheets of Dural had lost some of their initial strength so the factory needed its own annealing plant to treat every part as one of the last jobs before fitting.

Anodising involved plunging the parts into a chemical bath and passing an electrical current through it to deposit a coating which prevented corrosion. The electroplating worked in a similar way and was used to coat nuts and bolts in cadmium, handles were nickel plated and even tin plating could be carried out if necessary. It was one of the more vital departments and, as a result, the shifts were longer than in other departments.

Electroplater Eva Storrow recalled how the women on the shop floor were allowed home at lunchtime on Saturdays.

"I had to keep going until tea time to make sure there were enough parts for the men working on Sunday," she said. "The factory worked seven days a week with night shifts as well. For us it was a 7.30am start and out at 7pm - it was a long day."

Cigarette lighters:
It is said that
the British aircraft
industry made more
lighters than aircraft.
The Windermere
factory was no
exception. The two
main types were those
carved from solid
blocks of scrap
aluminium and those
made from short
lengths of tube - either
brass or Chrome
plated.

The foreman in charge of the electroplating section, Mr. G. Angus, rushed in one day to announce that all the fish in the beck running through the factory site were dead. A hydrochloric acid tank had been emptied into the drains that led to the beck. The next time the job needed doing, the acid had to be carried up onto a nearby bank and emptied across the bank.

A bigger problem occurred one morning when Mrs. Storrow returned to work to find steam billowing from her room and firemen standing anxiously outside.

"I had 26 taps to turn off each night before I went home. They were for the water, steam, electricity and so on. The walls were covered in pipes. That night I had missed one of them. The firemen thought the acid bath was boiling and would not go in. There was steam everywhere but it was only water with steam coming off it. I went in and turned the tap off. A quarter of a hour later it was back to cold water and when the inspector came round he couldn't find anything wrong!"

The strong chemicals caused problems for the workers. Overalls soon became pinholed and ragged and occasionally there were more serious problems.

Anodiser Olive Mayor got a piece of cadmium inside her glove once causing bad burning and blistering. Thorough washing with cold water saved it but one young lad got anodising acid into a cut in his hand and became very ill for some time as a result.

Occasionally one or two "unofficial" items were brought into to be electroplated and, if senior management happened to wander in, they were rapidly dunked into the various solutions to hide them.

It was often said that during the war the aircraft industry in Britain produced far more cigarette lighters than aircraft. Indeed, a cartoon at the time showed workers at Bloggs Cigarette Lighter Company beavering away on a fighter aircraft while a worker ran over shouting "Quick, hide the aircraft, the boss is coming."

Windermere was no exception. A great many personal items were made and management generally turned a blind eye so long as it was done in lunchtimes and scrap material was used.

Small model fighter aircraft on stands demonstrated the high skill of the craftsmen, while letter knives, pokers, toasting forks made from aileron rods and even tiny copper Spitfires made from pennies were all turned out.

The handles on pokers and letter knives were distinctive. Pieces of bakelite, plastic and perspex were drilled and threaded onto a bolt. With the bolt fixed to a drill, it could be spun against a file to produce a multicoloured, rounded handle. Many houses in Windermere had pokers with the "Short Brothers handles" at some time after the war. Candlesticks could be turned from blocks of Dural with a hexagon nut in the end to hold the candle.

The official attitude to this black market production was highlighted when Bill Harrison was caught by a foreman with nothing to do. Waiting for parts before he could do his next task, he was caught sitting idle.

"I told him there was nothing for me to do and he said 'well clear off and get a cigarette lighter made and don't let me catch you doing nothing again'!"

The cigarette lighters were made in two main types - either in tubes of steel or brass or carved into a block of aluminium. The tubes were just the right size for a sixpence to be used to seal the ends. The lighters carved from blocks of Dural required precision to make the top fit well but it was not a problem for those trained to build to an aircraft's close tolerances. Hardened steel wheels were made for the lighters, sometimes by slicing up a steel file which had become too worn for further use. When the RAF visited the factory, delivering or collecting aircraft, the first thing they did was to head straight for the machine shop for bits to repair their own lighters.

There were few in the factory not involved in some way. Inspector Nick Holt was presented with a table-top lighter made in Dural and wood by the machine shop inspector Sam Sears.

The factory manager's son, Peter Greetham, salvaged a piece of wing spar from a scrapped aircraft, carefully filled in the rivet holes, cut it to shape and polished it to make a superb book end. His father had to turn a blind eye because he had asked for one of the workers to weld pieces of aileron rod together to make Chinese rings for the conjuring act he did in his spare time. On the first occasion he was handed the completed ring he immediately threw it across the workshop. When the weld broke he asked for it to be done again. The next time the weld held up.

Inevitably some went a little bit too far with the things they made. A chargehand in the machine shop was said to have made an ironing board for his wife which was obviously too large to be carried surreptitiously out of the main gate. Instead, it was sneaked to the high fence surrounding the site and thrown over. Unfortunately it nearly hit a passing policeman who took it to Shorts police at the gate. They found the owner and made him pay for all the parts he had used to make it.

The most blatant use of Shorts property was by a panel beater who worked in the hangar, as recalled by Bill Morgan:

"The panel beater used to come to work every day on his motorbike and park it near the hangar. One day he came to work with a spare wheel over his arm and the police on the gate thought nothing of it. But when he left that evening he was riding a motorcycle and sidecar!

"He had made the whole thing in the hangar, paneled with aircraft aluminium and even with little perspex screens. The only thing which surprised me is that nobody built themselves an aircraft."

Model Fighter:
The craftmanship
of the factory was
shown in items made
in spare time such as
this model of a fighter
aircraft, given to one
of the lady workers.
Marjorie Winston

Made in Windermere:
some items made
in the factory, a book
end made from part
of a Sunderland wing
spar, a cigarette lighter
and a letter knife.
Peter Greetham

Opoosite top photo:

*Fuselage Top: The top
board holds the frames
in place while
the fuselage is built up.*

Peter Greetham

Building and testing

The Sunderland is a big aircraft. It housed its crew of 12 to 15 with space, if not actual comfort, within a double decked hull which even included a galley, ward room and toilet. Weighing up to 58,000 lb fully loaded (over 25 tons)[1] there were few situations where it would look small - except the new hangar built at Windermere.

By April 1942 the hangar was complete and shortly afterwards, looking like a beached whale, the first fuselage was towed gingerly across the factory site and into the new building.

Short Brothers had every right to be proud of their new hangar. As befits one of the world's leading aircraft manufacturers at the time, it was an impressive structure measuring 300 by 250 feet.[2] The hangar enclosed 75,000 square feet in a unique single span structure. The workers were told it was the largest single span building in Europe.

The Sunderland was not a small aircraft but that first fuselage, allocated the RAF serial number DP176, was dwarfed in the hangar.

In the rear corner of the building lines of steel bars stuck up out of the new concrete floor and around them a frame work of steel girders was being built. These were the main assembly jigs for the Sunderlands. The jigs were made at Chatham in heavy weight angle iron and formed to shape by the workers at Short Brothers in Rochester. Llew Llewellyn worked on the jigs at Rochester for Dumbarton and Windermere, before following the jigs to take up a new job in the Lake District.

When building an aircraft the usual method is to hang the frames in a jig and link them together with stringers. With this method a fuselage can be build in several sections, even in several locations under a dispersal scheme. The sections are only brought together for final assembly.

With a flying boat though it is the boat element of the design that dominates the production technique. The keel is laid in the jigs and everything else is built up from that. It follows that the only section of the fuselage which can be built separately is the tail end of the fuselage, built in its own jigs in the detail shop and bolted into place later.

The keel was made of an assembly of detailed parts. The jigs for assembling the fuselage were a huge steel framework but at the heart of it were the keel boards. These were assembled carefully into the right position and could be dismantled to allow the fuselage to be freed. Above the fuselage was another batten, the profile board to hold the top of the fuselage frames. There were also two other guides on each side.

The keel sections were laid and clamped onto the keel boards and then the frames were built up from the centre section outwards.

Opposite bottom

*photo: Keel Board: As
with all ships, a flying
boat was built up from
the keel which was
laid in the jigs first.
Here part of the keel
board has been lowered
showing how the jig
comes apart to release
the aircraft once it is
completed.*

Peter Greetham

The skeleton was gradually built up. The stiffener boys were next set to work to fix stiffening pieces - the stringers running from the front to the back of the aircraft. In the same way as with the tail section, the fitters cut and shaped the stringers before bolting them loosely in place. Rivetters fixed them permanently later. Then other internal brackets, stiffeners and fittings were added. Each was hand drilled, dimpled, anodised and painted before riveting. The frames or coamings of the portholes, doors and other openings were all jig built and installed into the frame before plating started.

A feature of the Sunderland's design was the ease with which it could be built. Panels mostly only had simple curves, reducing the need for highly skilled panel beaters. The exception

---

1   Jane's All the World's Aircraft, 1945/46. Sampson, Low Marston and Company

2   Short Brothers Rochester and Bedford Ltd, local objections to the factory premises, Windermere. The National Archives AVIA 15/3622

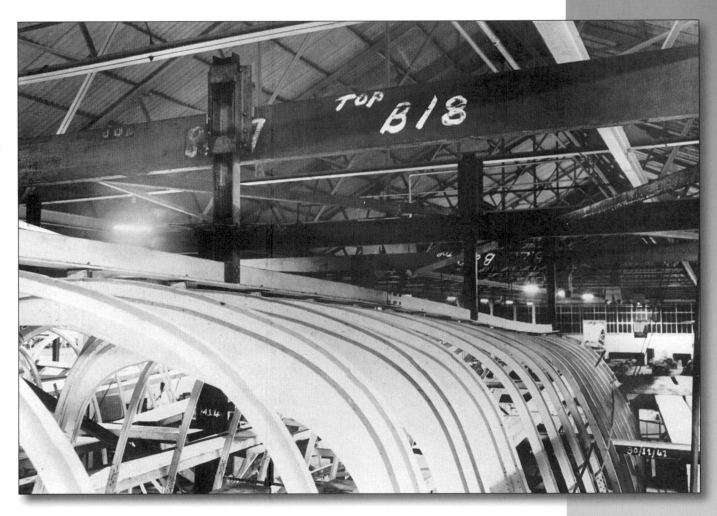

Temporary Panelling: Looking almost like a work of art, the detail of the structure of the Sunderland is clear is this fine photograph. The panels of the starboard side are fitted and then held in place with pins until the rivetters complete the job.

Peter Greetham

Three in Jigs: Skeletal fuselages in the jigs show the stages of contructions from the fitting of stringers to final plating. Note the panels have been trial fitted with temporary pins.

Peter Greetham

was at the nose where the stringers all tapered to a point and shaping the panels to fit was more complicated.

As soon as part of the hull had its ribs and stringers in place, panelling would start, even while stringers were still being fitted further along the fuselage. The panelling was a labour intensive process. A sheet of Dural aluminium alloy was cut to size and panel beaters would shape it to fit the hull.

The corners were drilled and held in place on the hull while the rest of the panel was drilled. In these pre-mechanised days, the position of each drill hole was marked out by eye and drilled by hand. No two rivets were ever quite the same distance apart, a classic feature of hand-built construction.

To aid the streamlining there could be no protruding edges or rivets on the airframe. The edges of the panels were joggled, rolled through steel wheels to create a stepped edge so when one panel overlapped the next the outer skins were flush. The rivet holes were also dimpled (countersunk) so the rivets were also flush. For each part of the process the panel was trial fitted to the airframe and then removed for work.

The final stage was sending the panel for heat treating and anodising before it was fitted with spring clips in the rivet holes, to be removed and replaced with rivets later.

There was rarely a moment when there was not somebody wandering through the hangar carrying a large sheet of Dural.

All parts were anodised before fitting as part of the military's requirements for corrosion protection. The panels were assembled with a barium chromate paste between the joints, sprayed inside and outside with zinc chromate and then primed before final painting.

Jim Dunlop was one of a team of four who worked on panel fitting in the hangar.

"When the tea trolley came round everybody used to down tools and head for the trolley. We used to be able to do another whole sheet of panelling while they were all waiting. We would finish the panel and then go to get our cup of tea just as the trolley was about to leave. We never had to queue."

The tea trolley was one of the most fondly remembered features of life at Short Brother's Windermere works, particularly the large piles of doughnuts!

At the height of the main shift the hangar was a scene of ceaseless noise and bustle.

The constant hammering of the rivet guns echoed around the building and could make conversation difficult at times. The riveting gangs followed the fitters across the airframe, removing the temporary bolts and clips and fixing panels in place.

The rivets were annealed to soften them and could be used for about two hours before they became brittle and had to be replaced.

The riveters worked in pairs, an experienced riveter operated the air gun while a dolly boy or dolly girl applied pressure to the other side of the rivet with small anvil-like hardened steel dolly.

The Sunderland did have some tight spaces where the tools would not fit, particularly at the rear of the step which had to be hand riveted - all the more difficult since it had to be watertight.

"We could not get enough pressure onto the rivets with the machines and the step had to be hand riveted," explained Jim Dunlop.

"They allowed us eight hours for the inside of the step and we could do the whole lot in one night. We did not get paid until the job was done. If it leaked we had to go back and do it again. Mind you they were not as thorough elsewhere. We got some in from Northern Ireland for repair and the work had not been as good."

Once the plating was advanced enough to create rigidity for the hull, cradles were put under key frames, allowing the keel board to be dismantled to give access to fit the double V section keel plating. The water tightness of the hull was

Tail Section Jigs: These steel frames were used to build the tail section of the aircraft's fuselage. Although work was already well underway on the fuselage, the timetable for buildng parts meant work had not yet started on the tail.

Peter Greetham

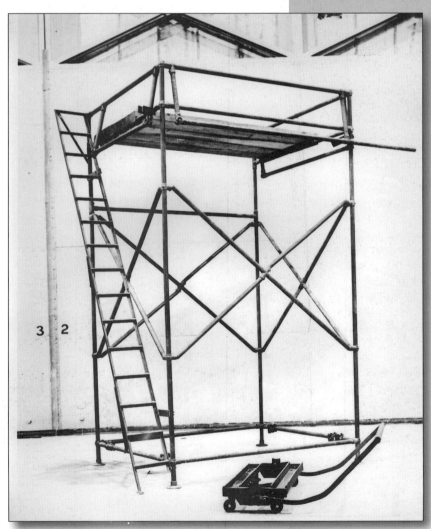

Windermere Scaffolding: The Windermere workforce designed and built their own scaffolding system which so impressed the management that photos and drawings of it were sent to Rochester. The sections were all welded with simple trolleys for easy lifting and moving.

Peter Greetham

Radio position: This jig holds the complete installation for the radios on the aircraft. They are the standard Marconi T1154 transmitter on the right and Receiver R1155 on the left as used on many large RAF aircraft. The intercom amplifier A1134 is on the left hand side of the desk. Workers recall systems being tested by broadcasting to an aircraft on the lake using call signs "Bowser One" for the base and "Bowser Two" for aircraft on the lake.   *Peter Greetham*

tested from inside while still in the jigs. The need to keep the hulls watertight and yet work with comparatively unskilled labour caused headaches for the foremen and chargehands.

It had been decided to put all the "green" labour onto one of the early hulls, as recalled by Llew Llewellyn.

"It was the fourth Sunderland, I'm pretty certain, which we put all the green labour onto. We had to knock out all of the rivets and replace them in larger sizes to get it done to a good enough standard. I thought it would never fly but the test pilot Parker took it up and never had any trouble with it. They did not even have to change the trim tabs."

Because of the strain of landing on water the hull was strengthened with heavier gauge plating and large rivets - normally 5/32nd. The rest of the fuselage was assembled with normal gauge panels fitted with 1/8th inch rivets.

By using unskilled workers, the main problem was the rivets not sealing correctly. The completed hulls were filled with water to test them before the interior of the aircraft was installed. The first aircraft suffered far more problems with leaking than was expected, until one of the draughtsmen came up with an idea.

Chargehand Norman Parker explained: "We used snaphead rivets on the hull which were countersunk on the outside but had a domed head on the inside. The problem was solved by one of the draughtsmen who said to flatten the rivets.

"The dolly was shaped to go over the domed head but if not held square the rivet did not seal properly. We made the rivets pan heads that had a flat top. It was easier to sit the dolly square on it and we had no more bother."

Production manager Bill Naiser had threatened to send to Rochester for more experienced staff but with a few changes, patience and guidance, the new workforce soon picked up the job.

Of course, having so many raw recruits around was too big a temptation for the old hands who had suffered the usual range of practical jokes that formed the initiation of apprentices in engineering the world over.

Nobody stopped to help the young lad seen so carefully carrying a brim full bucket of water with two wires sticking out the top. He made his way across the crowded obstacle course of the hangar, desperate not to spill a drop and not noticing the grins on every face behind his back as they watched him carry his precious bucket of electricity to its destination.

One day Stan Fearon was told the manager, Mr. Greetham, had asked for some mallets. He dutifully took three heavy, and dirty, mallets to the top man's office and, finding him out, dumped them on the desk and left. It was a long time later before he realised he had been had.

There was even a small notice outside the stores that said: "Wait here for a long stand". Only when somebody had been left waiting for perhaps an hour or more would the storeman ask if it was a long enough stand, and then send the red faced youth back to work.

Leaving sandwiches unattended over lunch break was a bad idea. Many returning with a cup of tea would find their lunch nailed to the workbench with a sheet of aluminium added to the cheese and pickle to ensure it stayed nailed down.

Bill Morgan started work at the factory straight from school at the age of 14 and was determined not to be caught out.

"When I was put to work on the engine nacelle I was told to go and get a dolly. Thinking it was a joke I refused and was hauled off to the foreman's office to tell him why.

"Later I was sent for some soft rivets and again I thought it was a joke and was back up before the foreman again. One of the engine nacelles got damaged and I was asked to get a rubber hammer. I was back before the foreman again. Then I was told to go for a jig and, well after that I went for everything I was sent for!"

The factory was a happy work place, even for those having jokes played on them. Talking to workers fifty or sixty years later many looked back on their days with Short Brothers as the best job they had done. There was a great pride in the work. When the factory switched from production to repair work every visiting aircraft was carefully examined and in most cases the verdict was "we would have built it better here", although no doubt similar pride existed at Shorts' other factories.

Part Panelled:
In the jigs, work is
well underway on
the first Sunderland,
note the panelling
has progressed
from opposite ends
of the fuselage.
Peter Greetham

Once completed in their jigs the fuselages were placed onto a boat trolley, allowing them to be moved around the hangar and then the fitting out began.

The wings brought up from Rochester and the tail from the detail shop were fitted. Other parts from Rochester included the floats and the fabric covered elevators, rudders and ailerons, as Windermere had no facility for fabric covering.

There was a wealth of cabling, pipes and controls to be fitted in addition to the internal flooring and fitting out of the cockpit.

The Sunderland was unusual for a front line aircraft in having so much space for the crew. They had rest bunks on board, a galley and wardroom where meals were made and eaten and even a toilet. Towards the rear there was even a small workbench for repairs to be carried out while an aircraft was at its mooring. All of this had to be installed along with the military equipment, the bomb racks which winched the depth charges out under the wings, the gun turrets and radar aerials - although the radar, still regarded as highly secret, was fitted at the RAF maintenance units.

The flying controls, as mentioned, were the responsibility of just one man, Jim Frearson, originally a cabinet maker from Kendal who had worked for Avro's in Manchester before being moved to Windermere. To concentrate his mind on such an important job he was told that he would fly on every test flight from the lake and, although he would be paid extra for it, he would have to cancel his life insurance.

"There were thousands of parts in the flying controls. We were not allowed to take the drawings home to study them but had to do it all in the office. I fitted the flying controls and Jock Shaw then fitted the automatic controls for the automatic pilot. He only put one set into a Sunderland and then he left and I did them all after that."

Fitting Wings:
DP176 arrived
in the hangar while
it was still cluttered
with scaffolding
and other parts as
work continued to
construct the factory
around it. The wings
were lifted by cranes
in the hangar roof.
The rails they ran on
are clearly visible.

Peter Greetham

Both had been sent down to Rochester to be shown how the Sunderland control system operated. It was there that Mr. Frearson was given some very useful advice.

"The foreman at Rochester told me how to make jigs for the controls. In the cockpit there was usually a big melee. Everybody was in there and they all wanted to fit their own little bit. The flying controls were in the floor and the people in the cockpit were standing on the control rods. Bending them caused severe problems but they did not realise how important they were.

"I built this eight foot wooden frame as a jig for the controls. I assembled all the controls together on the jig, all the rods, connectors, bolts and split pins were put in. When everybody went off for lunch I could get the whole lot fitted at once without anybody else in the cockpit.

"It was always stressed to me how important the flying controls were. An aircraft could fly if one engine stopped but if the elevators stuck in the down position then it went down."

The most awkward place to fit control rods and cables was the inside of the wing. Although the control cables were already installed when the wings arrived, each of the pulley wheels had to be greased.

Crawling into the wing, clutching a pot of grease, wriggling over ribs and in between the four spars was never a favorite job. When Peter Greetham was assigned to help with flying controls, being small he was soon given the job. He crawled into the wing clutching the pot of grease and also a pen.

"Most of the employees used to sign their names somewhere on the aircraft. While working on flying controls my signature was up in the narrow part of the wing where not many people went. Of course the girls left more than just their names. I'm sure some left their addresses too!"

The flying controls were not the only ones connected into the cockpit area. The Sunderland had a mass of systems for controlling fuel feed from the five tanks in each wing, operating landing lights, cooling flaps for the engines and the engine controls themselves as well as emergency systems such as the engine fire extinguishers.

The engine throttles were not operated by a cable and rod system but by hydraulics. The copper pipes were all shaped on jigs before fitting to the aircraft. Eric Mitchinson recalled how all the hydraulic pipes and fuel pipes were packed with a fine sand before shaping on the jigs to prevent them kinking. He also worked on fitting the controls from the fuel tanks through the wing to the flight engineers panel where the engineer could select which tanks to draw fuel from.

The cables were fitted with tensioning screws at each end, one left handed thread and the other right handed. Twisting the cable would then tighten or loosen both screws at the same time as necessary. All the stainless steel cables were spliced by hand.

"We had a lady there who did all the splicing of the cables. It was all she did and yet she still had long fingernails. We fitted the cables to a certain pattern in the wing and fitted locking nuts to hold them together once the tension was right. If the lever on the engineers panel did not go all the way back then we had to go and do it again. Woe betide the lady splicer if the cable was too long because then we would not be able to take all the slack out of it."

All the aircraft built at Windermere were Mark III Sunderlands fitted with Bristol Pegasus XVIII engines which developed 965 horse power on take off.[3] These were supplied by the Bristol company direct, and came complete with ancillary parts ready for fitting and connecting up. They were fitted with de Havilland constant speed propellers.

In addition there was a small twin cylinder air cooled engine fitted in the starboard wing root as an auxiliary power unit. It could be set to drive the bilge pumps and the refuelling

3 Bowyer, Chaz, 1989. The Short Sunderland, Aston Publications, 0946627 34 7

43

pumps as well as running a dynamo to charge the aircraft's batteries.

The radios on the Sunderland were the standard RAF fitment together with the associated rotary converters to convert the 24 volt supply to the 1,200 volts needed to transmit. They were also fitted with an intercom system between the crew positions.

A vital duty was testing the emergency radios in the dinghies. Peter Greetham was charged with running out the aerial with an earth wire dropped into the lake. By cranking a handle the radio automatically gave out a distress signal which could be picked up by a receiver in the factory. Unfortunately, it could also be picked up at Cark airfield where a full alert was initiated until the source of the signal was traced.

Working at its peak there were always four Sunderlands in various stages of construction in the hangar. The most noticeable feature looking at the hangar scene from a modern viewpoint is the lack of safety equipment.

Workers did not wear ear plugs against the noise of the rivet guns and hard hats were rarely seen. Slippers were provided for those who needed to walk around on

Camouflaged tail: DP182 was the last from Windermere in this green/grey camouflage scheme. Note the gun turret under the tail waiting to be fitted.

Peter Greetham

Fitting The Interior: Looking through the bomb doors on the side of the fuselage, a group of workers can be seen inside the aircraft.　　　*Peter Greetham*

the aircraft, but more to protect the Sunderland from damage than to stop them slipping off. Despite this the accident record was remarkably good.

There were minor accidents with the heavy machinery, particularly if clothing became caught in lathes. In one incident a girl managed to get her hand under the mesh guard on a guillotine and had her fingers trapped under steel pads that held the metal while it was cut.

For those who had come up from Rochester the health and safety provision were far better than they were used to. In Rochester the toilets were in the slip while Windermere had proper toilets and large communal washing areas.

One of the few serious accidents happened to the flying control engineer, Jim Frearson, during the final fitting out of an aircraft. Waiting to be launched, the aircraft needed only one small part adding to the flying controls and some final details painting before it was ready for test flying. The missing part finally arrived and Mr. Frearson dashed up to the cockpit to fit and check it. Finding it worked he ran down from the aircraft only to find the painter had borrowed the steps to paint the roundels.

"I fell about 18 feet and hit my head on a pile of steel jigs. In centre two they took a collection for a wreath. I was off work for a fortnight. It stopped production because there was nobody else on flying controls." Fortunately he quickly returned to full health and stayed at the factory until it closed.

The scaffolding around the aircraft was rudimentary compared with present day standards, although Windermere set a new standard by manufacturing their own, designed to fit snugly against the Sunderland. Although only a minor part of the Sunderland manufacture, so impressed were the Short Brothers management in Rochester with the ingenuity at Windermere that they ordered drawings and photographs of the scaffoldings to be sent to the other Sunderland production lines.

The initial recruitment drive to get the factory started up was followed up by a second hunt for workers to boost the number of experienced staff in the main assembly section. A large number of workers were brought up from the car plants in the West Midlands, particularly Austins at Longbridge who had experience of building the four-engined Stirling bomber for Short Brothers.

They brought more than just their skill with car and aircraft building with them however. The Birmingham workers also brought their union membership cards and a knowledge of working practices which were a revelation to the young lads from Westmorland.

Originally there had not been a proper scheme for paying bonuses on the main assembly work. Workers were on a low basic wage which could be topped up if a job was done ahead of the time allowed.

A number of the local workforce remembered there had not been a proper bonus scheme until the car workers arrived and demanded changes. They achieved their aim and a bonus scheme was created which enabled large amounts to be earned if the extra time was put in. Of course, care had to be taken or the rate fixers would change the time on the job reducing the size of payments.

Isaac Teasdale was working on part of the fuel system when one of the new arrivals asked him how much he was getting paid for the job.

"He said to me, 'Good God man you want more than that.' We had never heard of double time before they came, but afterwards we started getting double time for a lot of things. We thought we were getting experts from Birmingham up to help us build the planes but what they were expert at was extracting money from the bosses."

Unfortunately, despite their success at setting up the bonus scheme, the Austin workers were still not satisfied and the factory buzzed with rumours of a strike. They had been highly paid at Austins and were not happy to get less at Windermere. The main problem was caused when the hostel fees for their accommodation were deducted from wages

Bristol Engines: Bristol Pegasus engines were fitted to all the newly built Windermere aircraft. Note the maintenance steps in the wings on either side of the engines.

Peter Greetham

which made the pay lower than they were used to.

It was a sad episode because so many found working at the factory the best job of their life and the wages were so much more than had been available in Windermere before. It also attacked the essence of the camaraderie which held Britain together in the war.

Apart from a group among the Austins workers, there was little support for the strike. The trouble started in the hangar with a sit down protest. A circle was formed with oil drums and planks of timber where the strike meeting was held. AID inspector Elsie Kwaitkowski recalled how the trouble quickly moved out to confront the managers at the opposite end of the site.

"It was just the Birmingham crowd, not all the workers. They went from the hangar up to the detail shop. They formed a crowd outside and there was a bit of trouble on but it all got squashed."

Despite the lack of sympathy, the Austins workers kept up a limited form of industrial action with regular absenteeism for several months. Some were sacked for absenteeism and the rest never got the extra money they were claiming.

However, although the spirit of being part of a nation working and fighting together for survival clashed fundamentally with the individual demands for more pay, there was also a thought in the country at that time that the right to strike was one of the freedoms that the country was fighting for.

Despite the disruption, the production of the Sunderlands continued uninterrupted. As each aircraft was completed it was moved outside the hangar for engine tests.

Shorts employed a team who specialised in moving the aircraft around the site and any other heavy equipment such as the scaffolding. A Fordson tractor was used to tow fuselages on their trolleys and small Lister trucks were used to shuttle parts between departments. Consternation was caused when one of the trucks was driven into the ditch which runs through the middle of the factory. Although nobody was hurt there was some discussion about how to recover the vehicle from where it lay upside down at the bottom of the four foot deep ditch.

Moving the aircraft was a delicate job which could have disastrous consequences. Forcing the tail around too tight a turn could cause it to drop off the tail trolley. There were incidents of aircraft damaged beyond repair in such accidents at RAF squadrons, but the Windermere shore gang, led by Harry Wolverton who learnt his trade at Rochester, were very well drilled.

During construction the aircraft were lifted onto the beaching gear. A tail trolley fitted under the rear of the keel and two legs were bolted onto the hull under the wings.

The trolley was steerable and the main gear legs had swivel joints allowing an aircraft to be moved sideways if necessary.

The front turret could be wound back for mooring, creating an opening for the crew to reach out and pick up the mooring ropes, which were secured inside the mooring compartment below the turret. With the turret back and the two outer engines started an aircraft would be winched gently down the slipway into the lake, nose first. The winch rope was attached to the rear of the keel and once afloat the beaching gear would be unhooked, the air in the tyres keeping them afloat.

For moving the aircraft and ferrying crews about there were two boats based at the Windermere factory. Peter Greetham recalled that the largest was appropriately named Sunderland II and was the pride of the boatman, Jack Pinder. With its twin Rolls Royce engines it was capable of 32 knots and was used to clear driftwood from the lake before aircraft took off or landed. It also acted as chase boat when damaged aircraft were brought in. More normally it towed recently launched aircraft from the slipway out to one of the three moorings laid out in White Cross Bay.

The other boat was smaller and was used mainly for ferrying crew to and from the aircraft. It was named Mussel, after the small floatplane built by Shorts and in which Eustace Short died of a heart attack just after landing at Rochester on 8th April 1932.

The technique for beaching the Sunderlands required both good timing to catch the aircraft and strength to fix beaching gear and winch lines, as Bill Harrison recalled.

"We would have lengths of rope tied together and would be way out, past the jetties. The boatman would swing in towing the Sunderland from the front and he would swing

The Hangar:
The stages of assembly
can all be seen here.
At the front right
the aircraft is almost
complete while behind
it the wings have only
just been fitted to an
aircraft and props are
still in place to hold
them. The Sunderland
at the front left
is between these
two stages. Note
the Slingsby Falcon
Glider at the front
of the hangar by
the doors (see page 68).
Peter Greetham

the aircraft past us. We had to catch it first time, fit the rope and tie a bowline. They would be hauled by hand at first and then the winch would take over."

The beaching gear was floated out and fitted to the hull. The tail trolley was secured to mounting holes at the rear of the keel and the main legs to their pins under the wings and then the aircraft could be hauled up the slipway.

The winches were in the capable hands of the crane drivers. Their four ten-ton cranes could, between them, lift anything in the hangar. They ran on girders from the front to the rear walls, and one afternoon the temptation to see which was the fastest became too much. With two of the cranes backed right up to the rear wall, a signal was given and they were raced to the other end of the hangar - fortunately without incident and without management finding out.

A familiar feature for shore gang was the tame swan, Billy, who used to regularly visit the hangar. It was said that Billy could even recognise the bell announcing the tea break. Whenever the bell rang Billy would waddle up the slipway to the hangar looking for lefto-ver bits of cake and doughnuts. Peter Greetham recalled how one day some bright spark decided to soak a piece of bread in alcohol from the de-icing tanks for Billy. He waddled back down the slipway somewhat unsteadily to wash his mouth out with lake water. From then on he was a little more careful about accepting free food.

Once out on the lake the final few items were fitted as needed. The guns were one of the last things to be added, usually when the aircraft was on the lake. They were taken out of the store and degreased with petrol before being installed in the three gun turrets.

On a stormy day it could be a particularly unpleasant task. Sitting in the rear turret particularly, bobbing up and down with the aircraft swinging round the mooring buoy. It was a hardy soul who could accept chocolate cake from the tea trolley after an experi-ence like that.

The very last item to be added was the vice on the engineer's bench in the rear of the fu-selage. If not fitted at the last minute, they had a tendency to disappear, if not to some-body's home then at least to their workbench in the factory.

The final approval for any aircraft came from the government appointed inspectors, the members of the Aeronautical Inspection Directorate.

There was a team of six AID inspectors at Windermere, headed by Cyril Watson. Their task was to oversee all aspects of production from initial manufacture through to final as-sembly, particularly processes such as heat treatment of the alloys and anti corrosion treat-ment. They checked on the Short Brothers' inspectors and were even less popular than they were. The main responsibility was the final signing out of an aircraft, the last stage before it was handed over to the RAF.

The most important day for the AID inspectors, and the rest of the workers at the fac-tory, came when their first aircraft flew. For all those who had seen their first efforts at air-craft manufacture dumped in a scrap bin, for those who had struggled to make parts fit and worked so hard to learn a new and demanding job, the effort must have seemed worthwhile when that first Sunderland was winched down into the lake.

Short Brothers chief test pilot, John Lankester Parker, noted in his pocket diary that he travelled up to the Lake District on 9th September 1942 and the following day carried out engine runs on the first Sunderland, DP176, lashed down across the top of the slipway.

With everything in good order, at 3pm the entire factory staff were given the rest of the day off and allowed to gather by the lake to watch the launching of their creation. John Parker took the controls and started up both outer engines to help with manoeuver-ing as the aircraft gently touched the water for the first time. From the galley hatches on either side workers stood by with canvas drogues ready to trail them in the lake to help turn the aircraft as it was moved to its mooring.

The next day, on 11th September, Parker took the aircraft out across the lake, with an assortment of technicians on board keeping a wary eye out for problems. The full crew for that flight, recorded for posterity on the back of a photograph of the event, was: Chief Test Pilot, Mr Lankester-Parker; Asst Test Pilot, Mr H G Tyson; Chief Engineer, Mr A Manson; First Engineer, Mr J Hunter; Second Engineer, Mr C Sidwell; Electrical Technician, Mr S Gouge; Control Technician, Mr J Frearson; Marine Technician, Mr G H Lidster.

The pre flight checks were all passed and as he pushed the four throttle levers forward, Mr. Parker alerted everybody within miles that the first Sunderland had flown from Windermere. He also drowned out the cheering and clapping from the workforce gathered outside the hangar, who were delighted to see their first aircraft flying.

That first flight was only 20 minutes but during the course of the day another two flights of 30 minutes and 20 minutes were made. The following day a much longer flight of 40 minutes completed the test flying programme for DP176, and the RAF were instructed they could collect their first Windermere manufactured flying boat. It had been the first time Mr. Parker had flown from Windermere since his days with the Northern Aircraft Company teaching students to fly in the frail float planes of the previous war.

After his return to Rochester Mr. Parker wrote to his friend and fellow Shorts test pilot Pip Piper:

"The Windermere one went through very satisfactorily in four flights and was quite a holiday for me. It is 26 years since I last flew off Windermere."

Despite the length of time, he still had friends in the area, particularly Oscar Gnosspelius at Coniston whom he often visited on his trips to test fly the Sunderlands.

Fuel Tank Fitting: The access panels to the fuel tanks in the wings are still open while a ribbed strip has been laid to provide grip on the wing for workers. The aircraft at the far side (DP183) is almost finished.

Peter Greetham

Back ashore after that first flight Mr. Parker had kind words for the manager George Greetham and production manager Bill Naiser. He also called over the flying control engineer Jim Frearson and told him "this is the nicest Sunderland I have flown. I have never flown behind flying controls as good as these." An astonished Mr. Frearson was later told his pay had been increased as a reward.

The ease with which that first aircraft was accepted justified the efforts made to disperse production to Windermere and silenced critics of the scheme.

The process was run through again just a month later when the second aircraft was ready. DP177 was flown on a 48 minute test flight on 28th October 1942.

Mr. Parker was back at the lake in November to give some instructions to the RAF about collecting aircraft from Windermere. Wing Commander Derek Martin was the commanding officer of 308 Ferry Training Unit which had been asked by Coastal Command to collect DP177.

He recalled meeting the test pilot at the factory on 7th November.

"We discussed the problems of flying off Windermere, mainly caused by wind eddies around the mountains which created winds from almost any direction, often all at once! Apart from that the only hazard he spoke about was a small island in the lake with a house on it and I remember him saying to be careful not to hit the house. After many months of taking off from the river at Rochester where it needed full boost and maximum prayers to avoid hitting the bridge, missing the house seemed easy!"

Later that day he took DP177 on a two and a half hour flight to Pembroke Dock in South Wales, where it was assigned to the Royal Australian Air Force's 10 Squadron who were operating with Coastal Command.

Engine Test: Lashed down front and rear, the newly built Sunderland is having its engines run up and tested prior to being launched for the first time.

Peter Greetham

While most aircraft were taken to 57 Maintenance Unit at Wig Bay near Stranraer for fitting with items such as radar, 308 FTU collected several of the early aircraft including DP179 on 13th January 1943.

The factory quickly built up to their target of two aircraft a month and the test flying programme became a regular feature.

The test flights showed up a number of minor snags on the aircraft, which had to be put right. These were often engine faults or problems with the trimming of the ailerons and elevators. Engine faults would often show up during taxying and it was not uncommon for an aircraft to return without having got airborne.

John Parker did not have the test flying programme all to himself. Short Brothers, by the end of the war, had a team of seven test pilots looking after the testing of Sunderlands and Stirling bombers as well as experimental craft and prototypes.

Parker's papers from the test pilots' office show that Harold "Pip" Piper tested EJ149 on 31st January 1944 and Esmond Moreton and Tom Brooke-Smith, who was later to be chief test pilot, both tested aircraft from Windermere in that year.

Geoffrey Tyson, who moved to Saunders Roe in 1946, had visited Windermere before the first aircraft was ready taking senior managers from Rochester to see the works, including Sunderland designer Arthur Gouge and Francis Short. He also brought the prototype Short Shetland flying boat to Windermere on 13th January 1945.

It was recorded that the test flying programme at Windermere was to have been split between the pilots at Rochester and Belfast and it seems likely the Mr. Tyson as well as possibly George Wynne-Eyton and R. S. Gilmour would have carried out some of the test flying.

Afternoon Off:
The entire workforce was allowed to down tools and gather by the lake to watch their first aircraft being launched. DP176 was successfully launched and moored in the bay on 10th September 1942.

Derek Hurst

The snags highlighted by the flights needed sorting at the moorings - never an easy task where a dropped spanner was a lost spanner.

Setting trim tabs on a choppy lake was particularly bad. If the aircraft flew with one wing low or if the nose or tail had a tendency to drop, small trim tabs on the control surfaces could be tweaked to bring it back into balance. Grabbing one of these and bending it while bobbing past the tailplane on a dinghy was not a job to look forward to.

More popular was the company raffle for spare places on the test flights. After a couple of flights, an aircraft was fully loaded with workers to give an idea of how it handled with a full crew on board.

The biggest problem for the passengers was air sickness. Brown paper bags were handed out and on one flight, when a nurse went along, she thoughtfully took several dishes and towels for those who were unwell. Unfortunately she was the only one affected.

Stan Fearon recalled watching John Parker bringing one of the first aircraft back to the lake over Troutbeck. The lake was calm and still with no ripples to give the pilot a clue of how far above it he was. In these dangerous conditions he dropped the aircraft very gently bit by bit, feeling for the surface of the lake. He ended up well across the lake before the hull finally skimmed the water. On future occasions the fast launch was sent out to ruffle the surface for the pilots.

One of the few from outside Short Brothers to fly on the Sunderland was Cooper Pattinson, a highly regarded First World War flying boat pilot. He had been awarded the DFC for shooting down a Zeppelin over the North Sea. He also held the endurance record for flying boats in 1918 when he flew an F2A flying boat for nine and three quarter hours.

His son George recalled that, well known to Francis Short, he was invited on one of the test flights and John Parker asked him where he wanted to go. He asked to see his farms in Langdale and the 27-ton aircraft was flown at tree top height up the Langdale Valley, over Blea Tarn and back by Little Langdale to Windermere.

The test flights often took quite a tourist route around the north west. Passengers recall trips overflying Blackpool, heading out over the Irish Sea to the Isle of Man as well as touring the mountains of the Lake District. John Parker used to fly up to Cark airfield in an aircraft named "Dragonfly" and would also take the Sunderland at low level over the RAF airfield, scattering airmen on the ground to the delight of the passengers.

With the aircraft tested, all that remained was to wait for an RAF crew to collect the new Sunderland, sometimes to be taken straight to a squadron, but more usually to 57 MU's base near Stranraer.

Being the Lake District, the weather was not always suited to flying out new aircraft.

On one occasion, with the rain bouncing off the surface of the lake, one of the AID inspectors, Mona O'Neil, was having a last check over an aircraft before it was collected by an RAF crew, due to arrive the next day.

Everything was in its place and just as it should be. She climbed the ladder to the flight deck, glanced at the flight engineers panel and the wireless operators position and saw everything was ready. But moving towards the pilots seats she noticed a dark patch on the left-hand seat.

She saw the water splash onto the first pilot's seat and immediately noticed the leak in the canopy right above it. The RAF crew were going to form a very poor opinion of the aircraft and the factory as soon as the pilot sat in the pool of water. Quickly brushing the water off the leather seat she stuck her chewing gum over the leak and left to report the aircraft was ready to be handed over.

Christmas Card: A censored copy of the photo of DP176's first flight was issued as a Christmas card in 1944. The censors insisted that all the secret radar aerials were carefully airbrushed out before they would allow it to be used.

Mrs Ada Burrow

Test Flight: The first Windermere Sunderland DP176 takes off from the lake for its first test flight at the hands of John Lankester Parker, Short Brothers chief test pilot.

Peter Greetham

Living

Calgarth is the Lake District's lost village.

It was much more than simply a group of bungalows for the workers at the factory. It was also a community with a school, corner shops, village hall and its own policeman. Although it was only in existence for a little under 20 years, people quickly grew to love it.

Built at Troutbeck Bridge on land now occupied by the Lakes School, they were not particularly well built houses, not even plastered on the inside, only given a coat of paint over the rough brickwork. But then they had never been intended to last for long. Like the factory nearby, Calgarth lived with the threat of demolition from the day building started.

The village was named after the land at Calgarth Park on which it was built. There were 200 bungalows and a hostel for a further 300 people, together with two shops, dance hall, canteen, school and a small first aid hospital. However, it was its size on greenfield land in the Lake District that brought controversy and the Ministry of Aircraft Production had to deal with more complaints about their planned village than about the building of the factory itself. Right from the beginning there were calls for hotels to be commandeered and for lodgings to be found to house the workers. 1

Considering the Ministry was initially anticipating moving 1,000 experienced workers to Windermere, it is doubtful whether sufficient accommodation could ever have been found for them without new building.

Col. J J Llewellin, the parliamentary secretary to Lord Beaverbrook, the minister, outlined his own views in a letter about where to house the workers.

"If we get billeting then we need to cater for wives and children or we will not keep the labour there," he said.2 Llewellin was in favour of hostels and billets but did not

An aerial view of the village showing the bungalows in the main crescent. The school is the large building in the centre with the hall and hostels nearby.
Norman Parker

1   Short Brothers Rochester and Bedford Ltd, local objections to the factory premises, Windermere. The National Archives AVIA 15/3622
2   Llewellin Col J J , letter to Lord Beaverbrook 6-12-1940, in AVIA 15/3622 The National Archives

want new houses built. When the decision to build the factory was taken in December 1940, it was still unclear as to how the workers would be housed.

It was not until mid January 1941 that it was stated the village would be built. The 200 bungalows would provide married quarters, while accommodation for 300 single people would be provided in the hostel blocks. But then the arguments started in earnest. Llewellin was still uncertain about building so many bungalows. In May he wrote to his successor, the Right Honorable J. T. C. Moore-Brabazon, and said they should just build hostels. He asked for an undertaking to be given that they would not build houses.

Brabazon replied: "I will not have Windermere permanently defiled for all the world."3

However, a month later he noted: "The hostels appeared the same as the married quarters so there could be no objections to them."

It was even suggested that the hostels and married quarters would have a use after the war providing accommodation for holiday makers.

As the arguments ground on, the focus shifted to the permanent nature of the housing, as outlined in an internal note in the department: "There is no objection to temporary hostels, only to permanent houses."

Messing About With Boats: The cartoon cover from the Windermere Inspection Association's annual dinner menu.
Peter Greetham

Assembly Hall: At Calgarth village the assembly hall was used for a range of dances and other social events.
A G Winwood via Bill Harrison

3   Moore-Brabazon Rt Hon J T C, letter to Col Llewellin, 27-5-41, in AVIA 15/3622 The National Archives

Wavel Wakefield MP, who lived in Kendal and had property in the town, asked whether the solution would be to build the bungalows at Kendal where there were less controversial sites available.

Although Kendal was only eight miles from Windermere, with a train link, it was noted that the railway station was still a mile and a half from the works and workers would be tired by a long commute to work.

SHORT BROTHERS (ROCHESTER & BEDFORD) LTD.

Inter-Factory Communication.

Date __27/10/44.__

From __Miss Reneé Birchall__

__Stores Inwards.__

To __Miss Vera George,__

__Stores Records.__

Ref. __56/SS/4/RHB.__

Ref. _____

I beg to inform you,Miss George,that we are expecting on Saturday,28th October, or Sunday,29th October,at the latest,one Sunderland with crew,from Pembroke Docks.We have been informed that this crew consists of;

8 smahing-looking airmen,ages about 19 to 22 respectively,no older, and that we shall be flattered by their presence for about a fortnight,by which time we shall have no further use for them,and they will be allowed to return if undamaged.Incidently, it must be noted that the majority of this crew will be Australians,the rest of the said crew being divided between Canadians and English-men(This arrangement is made for the sole benefit of Miss George,who seems to have a preference for Australians.) If this crew is damaged in any way, i.e. loss of hearts the repairs will be charged to Miss George and Miss Birchall as said crew is the sole responsibility of the above-named.

If by any chance the above is not suitable to our purpose,i.e. as to looks,age,etc.,we shall not accept responsibility,and shall apply for a further crew to be sent down from Pembroke Dock by express Sunderland.,and will insist upon each member of the crew being the exact double in every detail to one of the following;

Alal Ladd,Clark Sable,Robert Taylor,Jon Hall,John Wyane,Errol Flyne,John Garfeild, Tyrone Power,Gene Kelly,etc.,

We shall require them to stay long enough to be at the dance at Bowness on Thursday next,for private reasons.not stated in this memo.

If this is all in order,will you.please confirm this memo. by signing your name at the bottom.

& oblige,

Yours faithfully.

R. Birchall

Your signature here. _Vera George_

Waiting for the aircrew: A joke memo on a Short Brothers inter-factory communication from Mrs R Birchall to Vera George.

Vera George

G. H. Bosworth in the housing department of the ministry wrote: "Their efficiency would be seriously impaired. Windermere is run by large hotel interests and they do not want their rich clients to be frightened away by the presence of a factory which may possibly make the place a target. Apart from flying and tests of the machines on the lake, there is no question of spoiling the beauties of the district."4

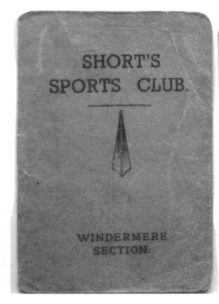

In June 1941 the Ministry of Works and Buildings, who were responsible for the design of the hostel and houses, consulted with the Friends of the Lake District over the scheme and faced their strong opposition to the building of any new houses near Windermere, opposition which continued through the whole planning process.

The Ministry of Aircraft Production, desperate to ensure that nothing should delay their project, agreed to give an undertaking that the housing would be removed "as soon as the military situation made it safe to do so", in the same way as the factory would be removed.

However, in January 1942, the wording of the undertaking was revised after a far sighted prediction of the housing situation at the end of the war. The houses would be removed "as soon as the military situation made it safe to do so at the end of the war and as soon as the Ministry of Health is satisfied that the housing needs of other parts of the country no longer make advisable the retention of this temporary housing accommodation in the Lake District."5

This foresight accurately predicted the desperate housing shortage at the end of the war and resulted in the "temporary" houses having a longer life than expected.

Initially the houses were to be built of timber, but the plans were altered because of a shortage of wood for huts and because the brick bungalows were thought to be better able to stand up to the Lake District winter. It seems likely the houses were all built and occupied by March 1942, about the same time that the assembly hangar was finished and the works was reaching its peak level of production. In August 1942 the Windermere Urban District Council sought tenders for the tenancy of the two shops. One was to be a greengrocer and general provisions while the other would be either a butcher or greengrocer and fruiterer.6

Perhaps it was because everybody who lived at Calgarth worked at the factory which helped to create the strong community spirit, or perhaps it was the layout, following a long crescent around the sports field and school. Certainly the village had a reputation for being a friendly and happy place to live - much the same as the factory.

Sports Club:
The Windermere
works kept up a Short
Brothers tradition
of having its own
sports clubs. These
are the membership
booklets.
Sheila Gudgeon

Calgarth Stage: Inside
the assembly hall.
The building was
used after the war
for teaching Jewish
refugees to speak
English.
A G Winwood
via Bill Harrison

4 Bosworth G H, letter to MAP, 20-6-1941 in AVIA 15 3622 The National Archives
5 Montague F, letter to Friends of the Lake District, 12-1-1942, in WDSO 117 - boxes 32 and 33 Cumbria Record Office
6 Windermere Urban District Council advert, August 1942, in WDSO 117 - boxes 32 and 33 Cumbria Record Office. WUDC

This was despite the fact that the houses were not the most comfortable places to live. They had single brick walls, rough cast on the outside, and thin felt-covered roofs. Some were built with three bedrooms and some with two. The speed of building and the rudimentary construction meant they were not without problems. Many of the bungalows suffered from damp through water getting in through the roof but many of the tenants worked hard to make them into homes.

But they had modern facilities, with inside toilets and a bath. The fire in the lounge was on the opposite side of the wall from the oven in the kitchen and they shared the heat.

The hostels were designed for unmarried workers, but many of the workers from Austins were put into the hostel while their families were left at home in Birmingham. Although 500 workers could live at Calgarth, there was still a need for more accommodation and some were put up in lodgings in Windermere.

Although supporters of building Calgarth pointed to the difficulties of bringing workers in by bus, there were many who lived in Kendal, Ambleside and even further afield for whom there was no alternative. The concerns about workers' performance were perhaps justified: the first bus from Kendal left at 6.30am and would not return until about 7pm to drop off exhausted workers.

The local bus firm at that time, Ribble, was given the bulk of the contract to bring in the workforce, helped out by other firms including the Magnet bus service from Bowness. At night outside the hangar a long queue of over a dozen buses collected workers.

The Ribble buses were part of their normal scheduled service but Bill Morgan explained that not only did Shorts workers have priority, they also had slightly cheaper tickets. Two queues were formed on the pavement by the bus stop. One was for workers while the other was for any other travelers who only got a seat if there was room. Further down the route, workers from villages nearer Windermere such as Burneside would find themselves having to catch the last bus, the only one with space left, which would bring a reprimand from the bosses if it was late arriving.

Being first out at night also had its compensations for a young lad, quick to get to the clocking off point. Being one of the first on the bus home meant getting a seat and, more often than not, one of the girls standing would look for a friendly knee to sit on for the journey.

The most unusual form of transport to get to work was used by one of the draughtsmen, who rowed across the lake every day despite having a wooden leg. David Newnham was a well remembered character who lived in a cabin on the far side of the lake, near Wray Castle and, no matter what the weather, he rowed across the lake and tied his boat up on the jetty without fail. One day he appeared on the factory floor with an unusual request. His wooden leg had become damaged and he asked the factory floor workers to repair it for him.

Although there was little spare time, Short Brothers did set aside some time for workers to enjoy themselves. In an effort to improve efficiency throughout the country, the government encouraged entertainments at work, building morale to improve productivity.

ENSA - the Entertainments National Service Association - not only performed variety shows for the troops, but also toured the armaments factories as well. Windermere did not miss out and not only received visits from ENSA but also the more high-brow CEMA, the Council for the Encouragement of Music and the Arts, which was the forerunner of the Arts Council, whose performances dealt more with classical music and operatic works.

The ENSA concerts, in the canteen, inevitably attracted larger audiences but, as Marjorie Crosland recalled, one operatic singer was upset that her performance was not being taken seriously enough.

"She was upset and, in fact they were all offended because they thought people in the audience were laughing at them. But what they could not see was there was a mouse sitting on a beam above the stage and running about right above them!"

Keeping to the class system traditions, Shorts had divided the canteen into two areas for shop floor workers and office staff. The concerts were all held in the larger section for the workers and the front couple of rows of seats were reserved for the staff and bosses. This gave the rest of the audience the ideal opportunity to heckle them as they arrived just before the performance.

Sheila Gudgeon recalled how the canteen was used for ENSA concerts once or twice a month and in between times for the factory's own version of "workers playtime", which also took place at the dance hall at Calgarth village. The canteen programme of concerts was organised by John Batty, who styled himself on Jack Lawrence and used the same stage name. He was based in the office and spent the majority of his time organising a varied programme of events.

A typical concert would involve a variety of performers from Short Brothers' payroll.

The band could be Al Rocco's accordion band, whose characterful leader was more commonly known during the day as Al Becks. Another dance band was organised by Harry Birchell, a saxophonist who had played with the Ginellers band before the war.

There was a choice of some very highly regarded singers. Joan May, who lived in Kendal, was particularly in demand at the workers concerts because of her fine singing voice. The comedian was Jimmy Ellis and even the factory manager George Greetham used to join in performing conjuring tricks, including a speciality of linking together seamless Chinese rings - all the more fun since they had been made on the shop floor from scrap aileron rods.

Of course, given a free stage and an audience to perform to, the workers playtime would, sure enough, turn to the production of Sunderlands as in this fragment of one of the songs:

"They say there is a Seaplane leaving our shop,

Its bound for the Windermere shore,

Heavily laden and heavy in debt,

If you ask for a bonus that's the answer you'll get."

Some of the songs commented on the origins of the workers:

"Some come from Bowness and Ambleside too,

Some come from Troutbeck - thank God it's a few!"

With the spirit of the evening established attention would turn to living quarters provided at Calgarth village.

"Short's palaces they have been named,

The walls are so thin,

Nails you dare not knock in,

You might give your neighbour a crack on the

chin,

The lady next door, she was having a bath,

When all of a sudden she sneezed,

She sneezed and she coughed,

And she blew the roof off,

And exposed what was left to the breeze."

Dressed for work:
Electroplater
Eva Storrow about
to set off for work at
the factory.
Eva Storrow

Hostel Home:
Joyce Harvey and
Martin at Calgarth -
they lived in a converted
hostel, one of which
can be seen behind.
Joyce Harvey

Quiet Roads: Pat
and Sheila Montague
playing at the bottom
end of Calgarth Road.
Pat and Sheila
Montague

Family homes: Mr and
Mrs Harrop and their
son George in front
of their bungalow at
Calgarth
George Harrop

Popular acts could find themselves on tour, as happened to a group called the Six Pin-up Girls. Although amateurs, they were well enough regarded to be invited to Cark airfield to put on a show for the RAF. Vera George recalled the evening: "It really was just a good laugh for us all but one of the saddest things we had to do was go to the Meathop Sanatorium. They were mostly TB patients and all had white robes on. It was very difficult to perform when we were so upset by the state of them."

It was at Meathop that they were asked to do something even more difficult: "We were approached and asked if we would do a show at Grisedale Hall, for the German prisoners of war. I said that I would not and the others backed me up. I don't think they would have been putting on shows for our men."

The prisoners heading for Grisedale Hall met an unfriendly reception while passing through Windermere, often booed and jeered. Despite this, there was some mixing with the locals including the occasional football match.

The sports pitch in the centre of Calgarth Village gave the Short Brothers Sports Club a tremendous asset, particularly popular with visiting teams who found it had the best changing rooms in the district. With Francis Short as president and chairman W. J. Smith, the sports club organised football, hockey, cricket, swimming, rowing, lawn tennis, bowls, darts, table tennis and card games for the employees at a cost of one penny a week, to be deducted from wages. In the winter months there was even some skating on a nearby tarn and some brave attempts at ice hockey.

Annual sports days were held at the Phoenix Centre in Windermere where teams from Short Brothers competed against each other and some from across the north west.

The Shorts football team did well, under the captaincy of Norman Parker who continued to lead the Calgarth team after the war, still composed of former employees from White Cross Bay. In addition to the local leagues, he recalled one or two more unusual matches.

"We used to play football against the German prisoners from Grizedale Hall, mostly naval officers. We also played against the guards at Ambleside - they were very good. We played against an RAF team but lost by 17 goals to one. Their left winger was Rees who played for Cardiff and Wales at the time but had been called up."

The RAF were a common sight in Windermere and regularly made use of the factory as a training base for crews. At one time, in early 1944, redundant Sunderland W3983 was brought to White Cross Bay for use as an instructional airframe with the instructional number 4603M.[7] Whether it was used to train the RAF or the factory workers is not clear. It was broken up for scrap three months later. The groups were booked into the Low Wood Hotel only a couple of miles north of White Cross Bay. They were marched to the works every morning by an NCO for their studies and then marched back at night.

Typical of factories across the country, Short Brothers' Windermere works had its very own "Dads Army" unit. The Home Guard had evolved out of the Local Defence Volunteers that was created in 1940. The Lake District had many units. In Bowness the Home Guard unit was given the responsibility of protecting the lake from invasion by German flying boats. To tackle this they mounted machine guns on a speed boat.[8] There were units at Grasmere, Ambleside, Langdale, Troutbeck, Windermere and Bowness.

7   Short Sunderland W3983/4603M, AM Form 78 (Aircraft Movement Card), Royal Air Force Museum.

8   Pattinson, George H, 1981. The Great Age of Steam on Windermere, Windermere Nautical Trust. 0 907796 00

The White Cross Bay factory had its own Home Guard unit with specific responsibility for protecting the site. It was always assumed that a German landing would be made on the lake and the works would be attacked first of all from the lake itself.

The whole site was surrounded by wire fencing and the Home Guard organised the night time patrols within the fencing, led by Major Howarth who worked in the production office. Richard Mooney was a member of the factory Home Guard.

"We had a rota of who went on guard duty throughout the night. We were put on a 24 hour duty watch. We did our ordinary work in the factory during the day but dressed in full uniform with a rifle under the desk. After hours we patrolled the factory and along the lakeshore. We were always told to expect a landing from the lake. The Home Guard patrols had long nights, but for the youngsters who were later called up to the Army, it stood them in good stead."

One man was patrolling down by the lake when he spotted a light out in the lake. Unable to get any reply from it he decided to take a few pot shots at it. No matter how hard he tried he could not shoot out the light. Eventually the shots brought others to the scene and one calmly asked why he was shooting at the reflection of the moon on the water.

In a more serious shooting incident one of the Home Guard men sitting in their hut was shot, a story which soon became rife in the factory, as Stan Fearon remembered. "Chunky Crammond was on the Home Guard and he was patrolling one night when he saw three people walking towards the canteen. Chunky challenged with the normal 'Halt, who goes there' but they ignored him and all he heard were some giggles. He shouted 'Halt or I'll fire' but they still ignored him so he put the Sten gun onto single shot and fired at the ground. The bullet ricocheted up, went through the wall of the Home Guard hut and hit a bloke sitting on the bed in the leg. Chunky got a real dressing down for shooting too low. He was told he should have fired at them!"

Wings for Victory Week: To celebrate the week in Bowness, this ladies clothing shop created a display of items made at the Short Brothers factory by local women. Items on display include the instrument panel, parts of a gun turret and an assortment of panels.
Peter Greetham

Football Team: The Calgarth team post-war consisted entirely of former workers at the factory. In the front centre (with striped socks) is Norman Parker, the captain of the team.

Norman Parker

Experimenting

The Sunderland was one of only a handful of aircraft to be in front line service right through the whole of World War II. But, to meet the changing demands of the war, it underwent significant modifications and improvements. It was a testament to the quality of the design that it was able to be continually adapted. Most of these changes were undertaken at Rochester but Windermere had its share of experimental types in the hangar.

The most obvious change to the production aircraft at Windermere was camouflage. The early Sunderlands all had an overall camouflage scheme of Extra Dark Sea Grey and Dark Slate Grey that was used for the first few built at Windermere up to DP182. A photograph (see page 49) shows that the next in the sequence, DP183, had a mostly white camouflage scheme, planned to blend better into the sky over water when viewed from a U-Boat. The upper surfaces were still initially painted in the two colour camouflage but later changed to a single colour, Extra Dark Sea Grey. The camouflage closely mimicked that perfected long before by seagulls.

Another distinctive feature of the Sunderland was the "stickle-back" array of radar aerials along the top of the fuselage. Although some censored photographs of DP176 show it without radar aerials (see page 53), all the Windermere Sunderlands were initially fitted with the ASV III radar system. An improved system followed that was fitted to some Mk III and all Mk V Sunderlands, with the array of aerials replaced with streamlined blisters under each wing.

Shetland Arrival:
The prototype
of the planned
replacement for
the Sunderland sweeps
in over the hangar.
  Peter Greetham

Armament changes played a significant role in the development of the Sunderland, always portrayed as one of the best armed aircraft in the RAF. The first Windermere Sunderlands had protection from three gun turrets. The rear one had four 0.303 inch machine guns while the mid-upper and front turrets each carried a pair of the same calibre guns. Even this was not thought to be sufficient when formations of long range fighters tackled Sunderlands over the Bay of Biscay and when U-Boats, heavily armed with flak guns, were ordered to stay on the surface and fight it out with attacking aircraft.

To meet the U-Boat threat four fixed 0.303 Brownings were added to the nose of the aircraft, controlled by the pilot. An additional free-mounted 0.5 inch Browning was used by the co-pilot. To protect against enemy fighters, two additional guns were mounted in the galley windows to protect the areas under the wings which the upper turret could not cover.

It is often stated that the Sunderland was given the nickname *Fliegende Stachelshwein* - "Flying Porcupine"[1] by the German fighter pilots who had learnt to treat this well armed giant with great respect. But curiously, the name seems to have been given prior to the main battles between the Sunderlands and German fighters. There had been a few encounters between Sunderlands and German fighters over the North Sea early in the war. But the fiercest battles with the German long-range Ju88 fighters took place over the Bay of Biscay in 1943. However, the "Flying Porcupine" nickname was already in print in an official booklet, "Coastal Command", that was published in 1942[2]. It seems more likely that the name was a product of British propaganda rather than German respect. However,

Weighbridge:
The weighbridge
in the hangar
was the reason
the Shetland came to
Windermere for its
final weighing and
centre of gravity tests
Bombardier
via Derek Hurst

1   Bowyer Chaz, 1976. Sunderland at War 1976, Ian Allan Ltd. 0 7110 0665 2

2   Coastal Command - the Air Ministry Account of the part played by Coastal Command in the Battle of the Seas 1939-1942, 1942. HMSO.

Single Prototype: The Shetland which visited Windermere was the only one of its type built. Short Brothers later built a second civil version but it did not attract customers.

Peter Greetham

Sunderland Replacement?: The Sunderland proved to be too good for the Shetland to replace it.

Peter Greetham

it's origins still paid tribute to the high level of defensive armament on the Sunderland compared to its contemporaries in the RAF.

All of these official modifications were added to the production Sunderlands at Windermere as necessary. Plans were modified and issued to the works and the final Windermere aircraft left the factory with the nose guns and galley mountings already in place.

There were some more radical changes which arrived at Windermere. One Sunderland turned up at Windermere with a large cannon fitted to the front turret. The factory inspectors were concerned about the turret leaving the aircraft under the force of recoil. The turret mounting ring was considerably strengthened. It is known cannon-fitted Sunderlands were under trial at the Marine Aircraft Experimental Establishment on the Clyde but it never became an official part of the aircraft's armament.

More radical, but seriously considered for a time, was the plan to use Sunderlands to drop miniature submarines in the Norwegian fjords where German battleships were moored and posing a serious risk to the Arctic convoys.[3]

The Marine Aircraft Experimental Establishment at Helensburgh on the Clyde worked on the plans to fit a pair of two man Chariot submarines to the sides of a Sunderland. It was hoped to drop them within ten miles of the battleship Tirpitz allowing them to lay warheads under the hull and disable the ship.

Six Sunderlands held in reserve at 57 MU at Wig Bay were modified and it seems that at least one may have had work done at Windermere. JM714 had been at MAEE Helensburgh and came to Windermere 'for mods' on 3 November 1944 (See page 145).

The miniature submarine project had many difficulties, not least the weight of the Chariots, each of which was more than twice the Sunderland's normal bomb load. With the Sunderland crews not wanting to stop engines in enemy waters, dropping off and recovering crews for the Chariots were major headaches and before the problems were solved the Tirpitz was moved north, out of range of the Sunderlands.

Alongside the creative and attention grabbing ideas, there was also traditional development work of bringing out bigger and better aircraft.

Windermere's hangar had been designed to accommodate the next generation of flying boats and, although the prototype was built at Rochester, Short Brothers did send their secret replacement for the Sunderland north.

The Short Shetland was the largest flying boat built in Britain at that time.[4] It had always been planned that it would have been built at the Windermere hangar if the RAF had ordered the aircraft. Sunderland production was two a month while the works would have built one Shetland a month.

In 1938, even before the war had started, studies of possible replacements for the Sunderland had begun. They eventually led to specification R.14/40 for the flying boat. Because of the scale of the project, the two major flying boat manufacturers were asked to cooperate on the Shetland design, with Saunders Roe designing and building the wings while Short Brothers were responsible for the rest of the aircraft. Shorts chief designer, Arthur Gouge, was in overall charge.

It was a massive undertaking to produce an aircraft with an all up weight of 125,000lbs compared with the Sunderland's 58,000lbs.

The first prototype aircraft, given RAF serial DX166, was assembled at Rochester in number 18 shop, the largest at Rochester. In a change from the Sunderland construction methods, the aircraft was built in ten prefabricated sections. Since 18 shop was too small for the completed aircraft, once the fuselage was completed it was rolled outside so the tall tail could be fitted. The wings, shipped up from Saunders Roe's main works

3   Hodgkinson, Vic, 1989. Beachcomber - the story of a Sandringham, Private.

4   Barnes, C H, 1967. Shorts Aircraft since 1900, Putnam.

at Cowes, were fitted on a concrete apron outside the workshop and the four Bristol Centaurus engines of 2,500 horse power each were installed.

But Short Brothers still needed to weigh the aircraft, not least to establish the correct centre of gravity. With the weighbridge at Rochester indoors, the only answer was to fly it to the only hangar designed to be large enough for the Shetland - number 20 shop, the Windermere hangar.

The Shetland was launched on 24th October 1944 and John Parker made the first flight with Geoffrey Tyson as co-pilot on 14th December 1944.[5] A full range of performance and handling tests were begun and after a few flights, Geoffrey Tyson flew the Shetland to Windermere.

The massive shape of the Shetland appeared over the snow covered hills surrounding Windermere on 13th January 1945, and it was initially moored in White Cross Bay, dwarfing the Sunderlands on the adjacent moorings. She was soon brought ashore and into the hangar where space had been cleared for her.

With the prototype still strictly secret, only those who needed to be present were allowed in but many managed to sneak a glimpse of the new aircraft which they might have a chance to work on.

To calculate the centre of gravity the Shetland had to be lifted into a flying position. Peter Greetham watched it being lifted with a strop under the tail so the cranes could lift the rear of the aircraft so the tail was almost touching the hangar roof. The crane driver had to leave his machine in place and climb down through all the roof trusses.

After its brief visit the Shetland left for Rochester, leaving its thunderous roar echoing around the mountains. It was to have a short-lived career.

In addition to replacing the Sunderland, other proposed uses for the Shetland had been as transport, airliner for BOAC, and a freighter.[6] All options were pursued but no orders came forward.

The planned production of Shetlands at Windermere had been proposed to start in July 1944 but was put back to December.[7] By the time of the Shetland's visit the factory was involved in repair of battle damaged and war weary aircraft, and the future for the Shetland was already uncertain.

The initial plan had been for ten aircraft to be built at Windermere between July 1944 and April 1945. The government had looked at expanding production but accepted that Rochester was not suitable unless new and expensive buildings were put up. Short and Harland at Belfast might have built the aircraft where there was more labour available but the works were said to be more prone to strikes.[8]

However, the order did not go ahead and it was decided the Sunderland was simply too good at its job to be replaced by the Shetland. RAF Transport command said they would like to order six Shetlands to use in the transport role, but discussions dragged on past VE and VJ days.

By that time it was already planned to close the Windermere factory and orders for the Shetland could not save the factory. Short Brothers had looked at ways of putting the Shetland into production after the war and one of these was to use the Windermere hangar – by dismantling it and moving the building to Rochester.

The plans to build the Shetland had gone much further than just discussions. The drawings had certainly arrived in Windermere and many workers remember seeing some of the jigs for the Shetland. Parts were ordered through the production office and

5   Barnes, C H. ibid

6   Shetland I flying boat. Official flying trials, 1942-1946. AVIA 15/1740 The National Archives,.

7   Shetland flying-boat: Flying-boat development 1943 May - 1945 Dec. Air 20/3140 The National Archives,.

8   Shetland flying-boat: Flying-boat development 1943 May -1945 Dec. ibid

Secret Visit: The Shetland was still secret when it came to Windermere and few workers were given clearance to see the aircraft.

Flying Home: When it left Windermere the Shetland underwent a series of RAF tests and evaluations until finally burnt out in an accidental fire at its moorings.

some even talked of some production starting, although there is no other evidence of such work.

Many workers recalled the Shetland plans were dropped at about the time of Sir Stafford Cripps' visit to Windermere and he may have made the announcement during that visit.

Discussion of the future of the Shetland continued post war, without reference to Windermere. The talks centred on whether there was a role for the aircraft and how much it would cost. Eventually, at an Air Council meeting on 12th December 1945 it was decided not to purchase the Shetland for the RAF.[9] It also effectively meant the end was in sight for RAF flying boats, even though the Sunderlands would survive for some time to come.

DX166 continued in testing at Felixstowe but on the 28th January 1946 fire broke out on board. Two leading aircraftsmen had been left on board as a guard while the aircraft was at its mooring. To make some cocoa in the early hours the auxiliary generators were started but the cooling air shutters were not open and the generator caught fire. The Shetland burnt down to the waterline and sank in 25 feet of water before fire crews could get to it.[10]

A more marked contrast with the Shetland could scarcely be found than the tiny experimental flying boat which took to the skies above Windermere to set a British first for aviation on the lake. While the Shetland towered over the Sunderland moored alongside it in White Cross Bay, the tiny Slingsby Falcon glider was barely noticeable alongside the flying boats in Short Brothers hangar.

Ready for Launch:
The newly converted
glider appeared
tiny, waiting on
the Sunderland
slipway to be launched
into White Cross Bay.
Lakeland Arts Trust

9   Shetland flying-boat: Flying-boat development 1943 May -1945 Dec. ibid
10   Shetland I flying boat. Official flying trials, 1942-1946. The National Archives, AVIA 15/1740.

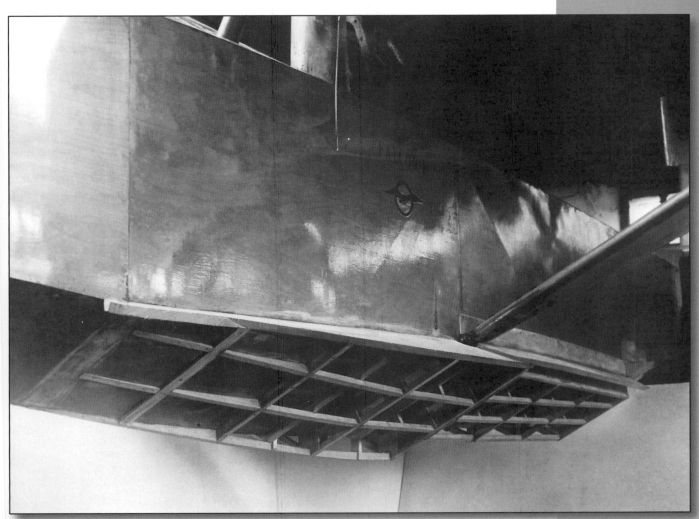

It wasn't originally built to fly from water but, when the Windermere Air Training Corps was given the aircraft, they characteristically turned to their lake as a launching ground.

More remarkably the aircraft still survives, hanging in the rafters of the Windermere Steamboat Museum. The founder of the museum, the late George Pattinson, was the son of one of the project instigators. After retiring from his family property business, George devoted his time to his collection of historic steamboats housed in the museum and could regularly be found polishing brass or cleaning boilers. But he also enjoyed sitting outside, looking over the lake and reminiscing about the glider and his father's part in it

The Slingsby Falcon I was built in the early 1930s as a landplane, under licence from the German designers. Only nine of the tiny open cockpit gliders were built.

When the ATC were offered the chance of their own gliders Windermere was chosen because it had pilots capable of flying the machine. Wavell Wakefield, the nephew of Edward Wakefield who had pioneered hydroaeroplane flights from the lake, played a major role in obtaining the aircraft. Wavell was a renowned rugby player who had captained England and had also served with the RNAS and RAF. In 1942 he was made the director of the ATC.[11]

Together with George's father Captain Cooper Pattinson DFC, head of the local building firm G. H. Pattinson and associated companies, he welcomed the glider to Windermere. With the support of Francis Short at White Cross Bay it was decided to do away with the wheels and make the glider into a flying boat. The simple idea was to rebuild the lower

Conversion:
The fuselage
of the glider was
adapted in the workshop
of local building firm
G H Pattinsons
__Lakeland Arts Trust__

11 Reason, John, 2004. 'Wakefield, (William) Wavell, Baron Wakefield of Kendal (1898–1983)', rev., Oxford Dictionary of National Biography, Oxford University Press, [http://www.oxforddnb.com/view/article/31791, retrieved 1 Nov 2007]

part of the fuselage to incorporate a flying boat keel and step and take it aloft towed behind a speed boat.

The glider was not taken to White Cross Bay but to Beresford Road in Windermere and G. H. Pattinson's workshops. Although more used to manufacturing windows and doors for the houses they built and having no drawings to work to, the joiners were under the expert guidance of Mr. Pattinson.

Foreman George Gibson was assisted by Basil Brennan in the building of the new keel.[12] All the new wood was obeche for lightness, covered with a skinning of marine plywood, obtained through the Short Brothers factory. It would perhaps have been easier to convert the glider by removing the landing skid and making a set of floats for it but Pattinson wanted a true flying boat.

When completed the glider was taken to White Cross Bay where a few more alterations were made in the hangar, under the shadow of the Sunderland's wings. The pitot head, which measured airspeed, was moved from the nose up to the wing so water did not enter the instruments. A bogie was fitted for launching and, looking tiny on the massive concrete apron, the glider was moved to the head of the slipway.

A chilly day in February is not the best time to fly a glider in the Lake District. However, Cooper Pattinson took the controls on 3rd February, 1943[13] and it was towed out across the lake behind a Chris Craft power boat named "Moana" and loaned for the occasion. A small crowd had gathered on shore including the men who had worked on the glider, members of the ATC and George, who was home on leave from the Royal Navy. He recalled that his father was only supposed to be seeing how the glider handled on water. He said the idea for the glider had been his father's and, as a result, he would not let anybody fly it. It was his project and his neck on the line.

Obviously impressed with the water handling, Pattinson waved on the speedboat and the crowd watching gasped in surprise as the glider took to the air. The little aircraft took to the air cleanly enough but as it tried to climb to gain height, the drag from the tow line pulled the nose down.

Pattinson struggled for height and then released the line. Once free the glider flew normally and it was taken down the lake, skirting Claife Heights looking for small amounts of lift to keep it aloft.

A safe landing and return to the slipway brought congratulations from everybody for Pattinson. The crowd knew the flight was the first time a flying boat glider had flown in Britain and they were all delighted it had been so successful.

Four days later, on 7th February, the glider was towed aloft again, this time with Wavell Wakefield at the controls. It was destined never to fly again. The reasons why have been forgotten over the years, and indeed so was the glider for a time. It was dismantled and taken back to the Beresford Road workshops where it was stored in a corner. Fortunately G. H. Pattinson were a firm who did not throw away things without good reason and the glider survived an age when many historic aircraft were scrapped.

When the Windermere Nautical Trust was set up to create the Windermere Steamboat Museum, it was suggested the unique flying boat glider should be restored and put on display alongside a remarkable collection of historic steamboats

Although it will never be under the control of a pilot again, the glider flies again today, suspended proudly above the boats forming the museum's collection.

---

12 Golden Anniversary of the lift-off of Capt. Cooper's unique aircraft Feb 1993. The Cumberland and Westmorland Herald.

13 Pattinson, George H, 1981. The Great Age of Steam on Windermere, Windermere Nautical Trust. 0 907796 00

In Flight: Two successful flights were made by the glider, towed aloft by a speedboat each time.

Seaworthy: Being towed across the lake, the glider proved perfectly at home on the water.

Repairs, conversion and closure

In January 1944 the order was given for the Windermere flying boat factory to be cleaned. It had to be made spotless. Corners which had not been looked at since it was built had to be swept. Brass taps had to be polished, rubbish cleared away and parts waiting to be worked on stacked tidily. Everything had to be made perfect.

The minister was coming.

Sir Stafford Cripps had taken over as Minister for Aircraft Production and on 14th January 1944 he visited Windermere. [1]On the surface it seemed another innocuous morale-raising visit, one of a number made by the minister and other government officials across the country. However, it marked a major turning point for the factory.

Sir Stafford made regular trips to aircraft production factories and component manufacturers across the country and during the war there were many of them. Guidelines were issued to factory managers who were told that Sir Stafford and his wife were vegetarians and teetotallers.[2]

On 14th January the minister's programme of visits included Rolls Royce at Barnoldswick and the Standard Motor Company at Kendal, on either side of his visit to Windermere. He also gave a speech to the WAAF officers' school at Windermere but not to the workers at Short Brothers. His news there would not have been so welcome.

Worn Out: Three battle weary Sunderlands moored on Windermere wait their turn to be moved into the factory for repair.

A G Winwood via Bill Harrison

---

1 Letters received following appointment as Minister of Aircraft Production, 1942. CAB 127/87 The National Archives.

2 Letters received following appointment as Minister of Aircraft Production, 1942. CAB 127/87 The National Archives.

The factory was in the middle of their main production run and working well at meeting the target of two aircraft per month. On the day of the visit Sunderland DP200 - the 25th off the production line - was delivered to the RAF at Wig Bay near Stranraer.[3] Sir Stafford may well have seen the aircraft depart. Inside the factory the next four airframes would have been in various stages of completion with another six keels laid in the jigs from the next ordered batch of ten aircraft.

The officials who accompanied Sir Stafford and Lady Cripps to Windermere included ACM Sir Wilfred Freeman GCB DSO MC along with Mr. Buchanan, Mr. Topham, Mr. Neete and Mr. Nash from the ministry.[4] They were remembered mainly for the way the party swept through the works, barely pausing as they were led through each sparklingly clean department.

"It was said he had come to see the place working but how could it be working if it was all clean?" was the comment of one worker. Some said the tidying of the factory interrupted production for about a week and then Sir Stafford breezed through not speaking to anybody outside his entourage.

But what most were not aware of was his more important private meeting with the managers of the factory in the conference room. It was then that he announced production at the factory was to stop. The six keels laid in the jigs were to be the last. No more orders for Sunderlands at Windermere were to be given and the factory was to become a civilian repair organisation (CRO).

The visit by the Minister may have been the result in a big change at Short Brothers barely a year before. Sir Stafford Cripps had come into conflict with the management of Short Brothers over the need to introduction mass production methods. The Sunderland

Waiting For Repair: Three Sunderlands moored on Windermere in the queue for refurbishment.
A G Winwood via Bill Harrison

3   A M Form 78, Aircraft Movement card for DP200, RAF Museum.
4   Letters received following appointment as Minister of Aircraft Production, 1942. CAB 127/87 The National Archives.

SHORT BROS. (R. & B.) LTD.

EMPLOYEES' TAX DEDUCTIONS RECORD.

Name_____0901____Storrow, E.____57_____ Code Number_____114

Week No.	Pay Day.	Gross Pay in Week.	Total Gross Pay to Date.	Total Tax Deducted to Date.	Tax Deducted in Week.	Tax Refunded in Week.	Week No.	Pay Day.	Gross Pay in Week.	Total Gross Pay to Date.	Total Tax Deducted to Date.	Tax Deducted in Week.	Tax Refunded in Week.
1	7 April						27	6 Oct.	4 10 7	129 1 11	20 13 0	15 0	
2	14	3 17 11	3 17 11				28	13	4 10 7	135 12 6	21 4 0	11 0	
3	21	4 11 8	8 9 2	12 0	12 0		29	20	4 14 1	138 6 7	22 0 0	16 0	
4	28	4 16 4	13 6 2	1 10 0	18 0		30	27	4 10 7	143 17 2	22 15 0	15 0	
5	5 May	6 6 10	18 13 10	2 8 0	18 0		31	3 Nov.	4 10 7	147 4 9	23 9 0	14 0	
6	12	5 3 9	23 16 9	3 7 0	19 0		32	10	4 10 7	157 18 4	24 5 0	16 0	
7	19	6 6 4	30 3 4	4 18 0	1 6 0		33	17	4 9 9	156 8 1	24 15 0	15 0	
8	26	4 11 10	34 15 2	5 7 0	15 0		34	24	4 10 8	160 18 9	25 12 0	14 0	
9	2 June	4 4 9	38 19 11	6 19 0	12 0		35	1 Dec.	4 10 8	164 9 0	26 7 0	15 0	
10	9	3 19 11	43 19 10	6 11 0	12 0		36	8	4 10 7	169 0 11	27 3 0	16 0	
11	16	4 16 10	47 15 8	7 8 0	17 0		37	15	2 11 1	143 11 0	27 11 0	8 0	
12	23	4 11 9	52 7 5	8 5 0	15 0		38	22	2 13 5	174 4 6	27 14 0	3 0	
13	30	4 12 4	57 0 0	8 19 0	16 0		39	29	3 8 6	177 13 0	28 3 0	9 0	
14	7 July	8 2 5	65 3 0	10 16 0	1 16 0	12/ Re	40	5 Jan.	2 8 9	176 1 9	28 0 0	10 0	
15	14	4 19 11	70 2 11	11 13 0	17 0		41	12	4 3 8	183 19 5	29 1 0	11 0	
16	21	4		12 9 0	16 0		42	19	4 3 8	188 3 1	30 0 0	13 0	
17	28	4 7 1	83 18 9	13 2 0	15 0		43	26	3 8 7	191 11 8	30 9 0	9 0	
18	4 Aug.	3 19 0	87 12 0	13 14 0	12 0		44	2 Feb.	2 8 8	196 0 4	31 2 0	13 0	
19	11	4 10 4	92 2 4	14 8 0	14 0		45	9	4 3 8	200 2 19	31 13 0	11 0	
20	18	4 14 1	96 16 8	15 4 0	16 0		46	16	4 3 8	204 2 8	32 6 0	13 0	
21	25	4 14 1	101 10 9	16 0 0	16 0		47	23	4 3 8	312 6 4	33 0 0	14 0	
22	1 Sept.	4 14 1	106 4 10	16 16 0	16 0		48	2 Mar.	4 3 8	216 10 0	33 12 0	12 0	
23	8	4 10 7	110 15 5	17 11 0	16 0		49	9	4 3 8	220 13 8	34 4 0	12 0	
24	15	4 19 7	115 6 8	18 5 0	14 0		50	16	4 3 8	224 17 4	34 17 0	13 0	
25	22	4 10 7	119 17 3	18 19 0	15 0		51	23					
26	29	4 14 1	124 11 4	19 14 0	15 0		52	30					
							53						

Form 805—12529/FAH/3/44

Good Wages: A wages card from Short Brothers, Windermere.

Mrs E Storrow

designer, Arthur Gouge, had been made general manager, but, being more used to ship-yard methods, seemed to lack the imagination to meet the Government's demands for massive scale production.[5] Sir Stafford implemented Defence Regulation 78 to have Short Brothers nationalised and brought under direct control. Oswald Short, the last of the three brothers surviving, retired and Arthur Gouge moved to work for Saunders Roe on the Isle of Wight - still involved with Shetland production. The purchase of Short Brothers went through on 23 March 1943.[6]

In charge of the future direction of the company, the Ministry of Aircraft Production had a wide view of what was needed in the country when they ordered Windermere to halt production and specialise on repair work. Only a few months later they were already

5   Barnes, C H, 1967. Shorts Aircraft since 1900, Putnam.

6   Consideration of future location of Short Bros. for government-controlled aircraft development, 1944-1945. AVIA 15/2126 The National Archives.

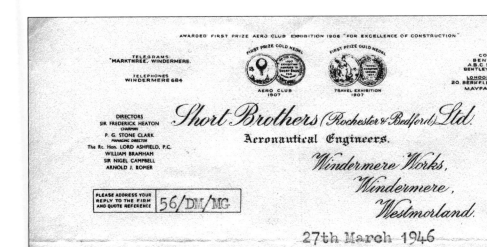

AWARDED FIRST PRIZE AERO CLUB EXHIBITION 1906 "FOR EXCELLENCE OF CONSTRUCTION"

TELEGRAMS:
"MARKTHREE, WINDERMERE."

TELEPHONES
WINDERMERE 684

CODES
BENTLEYS
A.B.C 5TH EDN
BENTLEYS SECOND

LONDON OFFICE
20, BERKELEY SQUARE, W.1
MAYFAIR 9541.

DIRECTORS
SIR FREDERICK HEATON
CHAIRMAN
P. G. STONE CLARK
MANAGING DIRECTOR
The Rt. Hon. LORD ASHFIELD, P.C.
WILLIAM BRAMHAM
SIR NIGEL CAMPBELL
ARNOLD J. ROMER

Short Brothers (Rochester & Bedford) Ltd.
Aeronautical Engineers.

Windermere Works,
Windermere,
Westmorland.

27th March 1946

PLEASE ADDRESS YOUR
REPLY TO THE FIRM
AND QUOTE REFERENCE
56/DM/MG

TO WHOM IT MAY CONCERN

Mr. Bertram Wilson has been employed by this Company from the 25th August 1941 until the present date as a Millwright.

We have always found him to be very conscientious and a good time keeper, and have no hesitation in recommending him for a similar appointment.

Had this factory not been closing down, we should certainly have retained his services.

for & on behalf of
SHORT BROS. (Rochester & Bedford) LTD.

G.P. Greetham

Divisional Manager.

proposing moving Short Brothers entirely to Northern Ireland - a decision as much to do with the political expediency of being seen to take jobs to the unemployed of the province as the size and modern nature of the factory there.

At Windermere the change also highlighted the wider issue of what Britain needed for the war effort as time moved on. Britain was always better placed for a long war than Germany. By directing effort into expanding industrial production early on, it meant by the middle years of the war huge amounts of weapons, including aircraft, were being produced. But as those aircraft that survived wore out, it was far more efficient to renew and refurbish them than to build yet more new ones - and so came the Government's idea of having a whole factory to specialise in CRO work for the Sunderland.

Llew Llewellyn was present at the meeting with Sir Stafford Cripps when he announced the decision. An elected representative of the workers and also chairman of the Shorts

Proud workers: A group of workers under a Sunderland. The group is thought to include Norman Parker, B Singleton and Bill Adams (2nd from right)

Peter Haslam

Tall aircraft: Dwarfed by their aircraft, a group of workers pose under their recently finished Sunderland.

Peter Haslam

sports club, he recalled how Sir Stafford explained that they wanted Windermere to specialise in repair work. The news that production had stopped probably meant the end of plans for the Shetland production at Windermere as well. Many factory workers remember that the Shetland plans were dropped after the minister's visit.

But the change to CRO work was going to cause problems. The carefully timetabled production of parts was set up so that parts were available as soon as they were needed at the assembly stages. With the last keel just laid in the jigs some workers were about to find themselves with little to do.

It was Mr. Llewellyn who spoke up and asked when they could expect the first aircraft for repair. He quickly explained the system where parts were made to fit in with the production timetables.

"I told him the parts were made to order. Girls made the bits, then they went on to sub assembly and then to the aircraft in the hangar. The girls in the top shop would have had nothing to do for six months while waiting for building to finish and for the first repair aircraft to arrive," he recalled.

With a different minister such a request might not have gone down well but Sir Stafford was a strong union man who preferred talking to workers than their managers. After a brief conversation he announced that the first repair contract would arrive very shortly. Indeed, the earliest aircraft so far traced arrived at Windermere for repair on 28th February 1944 - just a fortnight later. (See page 144)

The day after the meeting with Sir Stafford, factory manager George Greetham called Mr. Llewellyn into his office and thanked him for raising the difficult issue with the minister.

Under the CRO contracts there was still an over supply of labour at Windermere and many found themselves transferred out to other factories across the north west.

Trafford Park in Manchester was a common posting and the bomber production lines received a boost from the Sunderland workers. Some worked on the Lancaster production lines. One lady was sent to the Ford works making Rolls Royce engines for Spitfires, Lancasters, and the other aircraft using the popular and powerful engine. After six months training she was qualified as an acetylene welder working on the engine's inlet valves.

The move brought a very different lifestyle. In the big city much more was happening but the war was also closer. The city was full of men in the forces and air raids were far more common. Trips home to visit family and loved ones often entailed long interrupted journeys as trains were held up by air raids. Today it is barely over an hour and a half up the motorway. For most of those transferred to Manchester the chance to return home permanently did not come until the war ended and after the big VE Day celebrations in the city centre.

At Windermere the repair contracts also brought the war closer. For the first time the horrors of what the Sunderlands were doing was seen at Windermere, as battle damaged aircraft limped in for repair. On more than one occasion girls from the factory were banned from entering the aircraft until the blood was hosed from them.

Llew Llewellyn remembered the second or third of the CRO contracts was particularly bad. "There was a big hole in the fuselage which went through the radar operator's position and the operator himself. The girls were not allowed aboard that one because of the terrible mess."

Another Sunderland made its way to Windermere from Sullom Voe having survived another tough battle. Hauled up the slipway the damage to the rear turret was obvious and the hose pipes were used again to try and wash it clean of blood stains. It was a particularly unusual aircraft since all the information plates were in Norwegian. Most of the factory knew they had a visitor from one of their allies in the works.

Converting to American Engines: The Pratt & Whitney engines on the aircraft converted to MkV standard needed new engine nacelles to hold them. These were made in Windermere in these templates.

Peter Greetham

Sunderland W6030 had arrived from the Norwegian 330 Squadron on 24th June 1944.[7] It was classified as category B, indicating that it needed extensive repairs which could only be done at one of Short Brothers factories. However, after detailed examination at Windermere it was reclassified as category E on 10th July, which indicated a total write-off. The aircraft was broken up and scrapped at White Cross Bay. A similar fate befell several aircraft brought to Windermere when they were beyond their useful lifespan. Some were even ferried to the lake after being struck off charge by the RAF. Workers would set about the worn-out hulks with fire axes with the metal stored on a scrap yard by the top shop ready for reprocessing for the war effort.

Aircraft usually arrived with temporary repairs carried out by the squadrons to enable them to make the trip to Windermere. Some of the aircraft only needed minor repairs, albeit with specialist parts not available on the squadrons. While the detailed refurbishments were carried out inside the hangar, aircraft just needing one or two new panels were worked on outside. The assessments were carried out by the factory inspectors who undertook a detailed examination of what work was needed. Worksheets were produced for each job and parts ordered as needed.

The repair contracts brought some dramatic moments to the lake. On one occasion a beaching team was held back late at the works waiting for a damaged aircraft that was being flown to Windermere urgently. Word was passed that the hull of the aircraft had been holed and the two boats were standing by ready with the beaching gear. The pilot landed close to White Cross Bay and taxied at speed to meet the boats. The beaching gear was fitted with more haste than usual and, waving the beaching party clear, the pilot then revved up the engines and drove the aircraft onto the bottom of the slipway before it sank in the bay. When it was winched from the lake, water poured from the holes in the colander-like hull as the beaching party stood by, their next repair work plain for all to see.

Not all the repairs were to battle damage. Some were the result of accidents, as typified by DD866 which arrived at Windermere on 23rd March 1944.[8] On 4th March the aircraft was returning from a patrol to Pembroke Dock where the Australian 461 Squadron was based. Forced to land in a smaller than normal area, the pilot overshot on landing and the keel hit a submerged reef. The accident report stated that the pilot had been unaware the outer engines were not fully throttled back and were still producing some power which increased the length of the landing run. The result was another category B repair job for Windermere.

The repair contracts ran throughout 1944 until at least August, although there is some evidence of aircraft arriving later in the year. Then in 1945 a new type of work was given to Windermere. Instead of simply repairing aircraft, they were stripped out completely, fully refurbished and brought up to the new Sunderland MkV standard. The MkV used American Pratt and Whitney Twin Wasp engines but the same basic airframe as the Mk III, and 88 Mk IIIs were converted to the new standard.[9]

7   A M Form 78, Aircraft movement card for W6030, RAF Museum.

8   A M Form 78, Aircraft movement card for DD866, RAF Museum.

9   Bowyer, Chaz, 1989. The Short Sunderland, Aston publications. 0 7110 0665 2

One problem faced with the Mk III was the practice of running the Bristol Pegasus engines at combat ratings nearly all the time, causing them to fail too frequently. Engines with a greater reserve of power were needed and the Australian 10 Squadron suggested the 1,200 hp American engines, which Short Brothers initially thought would be too powerful for the Sunderland wing. Uniquely, prototypes were built by Shorts and the Australians, and both proved successful. The advantages were not just the extra power. Having fully feathering propellers meant the propeller blades could be turned edge on to the airflow when an engine was stopped. This prevented the propeller windmilling and greatly reduced the drag when an engine was lost. For the first time a Sunderland could still be flown with two engines out on the same wing.

The first recorded Mk V conversion at Windermere was Sunderland PP137, which arrived on 17th January 1945,[10] although there may have been others earlier which have not been traced.

The same process of detailed examination was used, but any part likely to be worn was stripped out and replaced, as were a significant number of critical parts. In particular, all the flying controls were replaced on all the converted aircraft. The new engines arrived packed in crates direct from the United States. Each came with a set of tools and those working on fitting them soon had their tool kits full with brand new spanner sets.

There were also changes to the aircraft's structure to make as well as repairs to any corroded or damaged panels. The mid upper turret was removed from the Mk III Sunderlands and replaced on the Mk V with two gun hatches just to the rear of the wings. The gunners had positions built into the hull and hatches closed off the openings when they were not in use.

Factory Fresh: A newly built Sunderland, inspected and tested, waits on the mooring at White Cross Bay for an RAF crew to collect her.

Peter Greetham

10 A M Form 78, Aircraft movement card for PP137, RAF Museum.

Final Aircraft: The senior management at Short Brothers Windermere pose in front of their last aircraft ML877, just converted to a MkV. Front row l-r: Mr Stone; Polly Cottrell, in charge of welfare, and her dog; Chief inspector Alf Peckham; Bill Smith; Manager George Greetham; Shop Superintendent Did Naiser; Mr Hunter; Mr Jones and Mr Moyer. Back row l-r: Foreman Jack Ritson; Foreman Bert Manson; Mr Tanner; Mr Goldsmith; Foreman Mr Cartledge; Foreman Mr Taylor; Joe Penny.

Peter Greetham

The number of aircraft repaired or converted at Windermere is uncertain since factory records have not survived. According to some of the workers there were about 25 refurbished at Windermere.

Immediately after the war an open day was held at the works and a report was carried by the Westmorland Gazette.[11] In the article the factory manager was quoted as saying there was an output of 2,640,000 lbs of parts produced at the works which equated to 59 complete aircraft - 35 new and 24 refurbished. The number of jigs produced for manufacture was 11,500 and the labour force had peaked at 1,571 in 1942. The total wages bill for the factory had been £900,000.

Since the factory records have not survived, it is not possible to say exactly how many aircraft were repaired, how many were refurbished and how many were converted from MkIII to MkV. Those aircraft that are known to have visited Windermere are listed in the appendices (see page 144).

The visiting aircraft brought an additional benefit for the workers at Windermere, particularly the women - each aircraft came complete with a crew of young airmen. Although some crews headed straight for the machine shop to have cigarette lighters repaired, others lingered to talk to the young girls.

Less popular was a group of American women ferry pilots who arrived one day. Dressed in smart navy blue uniforms, with bright red fingernails, these glamorous allies were looked on by the factory workers with ill-concealed envy.

---

11   Wage Bill of Nearly £1,000,000. Facts and Figures of Lakeland's Sunderlands. 9 Feb 1946, Westmorland Gazette.

There were some embarrassing moments when crews did not expect AID inspectors to be women. Elsie Kwaitkowski boarded the boat to meet a newly arrived Sunderland for initial inspection. The crew had climbed out onto the mainplane, stripped off and dived into the lake. Shocked to find a lady on the launch they refused to come out of the water until she had covered her eyes.

From available records it appears that the Windermere factory met their targets for production, especially while building Sunderlands. But the works was still somewhat at odds with Sir Stafford Cripps, who sent a memo warning that there was every possibility of the works being closed down if poor production performances did not improve. The letter was displayed on the factory notice board for all to see and was spotted by Bernard Smith, the navigator on ML877, when it was delivered for conversion.

But the factory survived until the end of the war in Europe - the closure coming in line with the pledges made when the works was built. On 8th June, a month after VE day, contracts for the conversion of seven aircraft were cancelled.[12] They had all been delivered to Windermere between March and May and were moored both in White Cross Bay and across the lake in Wray Bay. There were still aircraft in the hangar. ML877 had arrived from 228 Squadron on 4th April 1945 and the conversion to Mk V standard had started when the order to wind up the factory came through. It was the last aircraft to be finished at Windermere and once complete formed the backdrop for a photograph of senior staff on the slipway in front of the hangar.

There were nearly 600 people still working at the factory in June 1945, who were all put on notice at the end of the month.[13] By January 1946 only George Greetham, the factory manager, was left on the site as the final member of administrative staff.

It was the end of an era for industry in Windermere. Never again would heavy industry appear in the area and never again would the people of the Lake District have the chance to build advanced aircraft. Many of the workers stayed on at Calgarth but their landlords changed. Instead of paying rent to the Ministry of Aircraft Production, they paid it to the Windermere Urban District Council who took over the whole village.

For the experienced staff from Rochester there was a choice. Some stayed but others moved back to the Medway to continue with Short Brothers. Others went to Short and Harland in Belfast. It seemed that Northern Ireland was a better prospect as the government, who had nationalised Short Brothers during the war, decided Rochester also had no future for the construction of aircraft. The Seaplane Works at Rochester was closed in 1948 and all of Short Brothers production was transferred to Belfast. The company survived the many vagaries of the aircraft industry in the following decades and still continues in Belfast, although Shorts, as it became known, was taken over by the Canadian Bombardier company and is mostly employed today in manufacturing components.

For the workers who stayed at Windermere after the war, some found it difficult to settle into other jobs. Several set up their own businesses, but it was not just the fact that there was no work which paid as well as Short Brothers. It was also hard to recapture the camaraderie and spirit that epitomised life at White Cross Bay. Many 50 years later still looked back on it as "the best job I have ever had."

---

12 AM Form 78, Aircraft movement cards for ML815, ML763, NJ171, DP199, ML784, EJ151 and ML783 RAF Museum.

13 A Windermere problem – future of Air Factory, 30 June 1945, The Guardian.

Sunderlands at war

On 21st May 1943, after eight hours on patrol, the crew of DP177 - the second Windermere built Sunderland - saw a fully surfaced U-Boat just half a mile away on the port bow. This was the third time in a little over three months that this crew had found a U-Boat. It was the height of the Battle of the Atlantic.

The aircraft was at 3,000 feet and the pilot, F/O N. C. Gerrard, turned to get into an attacking position. The U-Boat dived as the turn was made and had been submerged for three quarters of a minute when the Sunderland reached the swirl where it had dived. Since the aircraft was reaching the end of its patrol Gerrard decided to drop four depth charges in the area "in the hope of causing some mental anxiety to the crew if not physical damage to the U-Boat" as was recorded in the squadron diary.[1]

It has been an unusually busy time for this crew. DP177 had been delivered direct to RAF station Pembroke Dock on 7th November 1942 and just after Christmas was chosen for a VIP ferry flight taking high ranking officers to Gibraltar, no doubt because it was still clean. The first operational flight was on 8th January and it was soon involved in very active service.

The primary role for the Short Sunderland was maritime reconnaissance. Typically this meant searching for, and destroying, German U-Boats. Each aircraft was equipped with eight 250lb depth charges. As the battle progressed, radar and flares made night patrols more effective but in these early years of the war there were few aids.

DP177 was again on routine patrol on 3rd February 1943 when the crew spotted a surfaced U-Boat 12 miles away.[2] The captain increased the aircraft speed to 190 knots but, while still just over two miles away the crew of the submarine spotted the aircraft and crashed dived, managing to be submerged in 15 seconds. Just under a minute later the Sunderland arrived over the spot and two 250 lb depth charges were dropped but nothing further was seen.

1   10 Squadron RAAF Operations Record Book, 1943 Air 27/152 The National Archives.

2   10 Squadron RAAF Operations Record Book, ibid

The other attack took place on 29th April while looking for an enemy surface force.[3] At 09.28 smoke and then a U-Boat periscope was seen on the starboard bow six miles away. As the aircraft approached it was realised the submarine was surfacing and, flying at just 70 feet above the waves, the captain, F/O Gerrard, attacked dropping six depth charges. The aim in such attacks was to drop a spread of depth charges on either side of the submarine, crushing the hull between explosions. Gerrard managed a perfect straddle on the U-Boat with the charges exploding on either side of it. An oil streak was seen from the submarine immediately after the explosion, although gunners on the U-Boat managed to fire back, scoring hits on the aircraft's wings and the cowling of the port inner engine. The Sunderland gunners returned fire. The aircraft climbed ready to attack again but then another Sunderland appeared on the scene - P of 461 Squadron, also based at Pembroke Dock, straddled the U-Boat with depth charges and it was seen to sink horizontally, then the stern emerged and it disappeared vertically. The crew considered the U-Boat was of the 740 ton class - one of the more common Atlantic submarines.

Unfortunately post war research has cast doubt on how much damage was caused by the attack. The U-Boat is thought to have been U-119[4] which was damaged. This is disputed by some post war research claims to show U-119 was not damaged but was sunk two months later by HMS *Starling*.[5] It seems that, if the U-Boat was indeed U-119, it had a lucky escape.

It was certainly unusual for one aircraft to be involved in three U-Boat attacks within such a short space of time. It was more common for the over-ocean patrols to be long hours of eye aching searching into the glare of sea and sky with nothing to relieve the monotony except tea from the galley.

Inauspicious Start: DP198, which went on to become the RAF's longest serving Sunderland, needed repairs before even making it to a squadron. She was ashore at Wig Bay near Stranraer when gale force winds toppled her, causing damage to the port wing and float. In all 13 aircraft were damaged: DP195, JM718, JM717, ML838, ML840, JM720, ML843, JM719, JM668, DP198, EJ167, ML842, T9109.

Henry Rolfe via John Evans

3 10 Squadron RAAF Operations Record Book, ibid

4 Wynn, Kenneth, 1997. U-Boat Operations of World War II Volume I: Career histories, U1-U510. Caxton Editions. 1-84067-525-X

5 Bowyer, Chaz, 1989. The Short Sunderland, Aston publications. 0 7110 0665 2

The intelligence officer from the Canadian manned 423 Squadron recorded in the squadron's operation diary: "Attacks on U-Boats, or even sightings, are so rare that a crew is seldom able to learn by their experiences or by their mistakes."[6]

It is all too easy for history to record the incidents, the brief moments of excitement that punctuate the long hours of boredom in a war. And when a Sunderland could be on patrol at 1,000 feet over an empty ocean for 13 or 14 hours, they were very long hours.

But the German High Command was aware of the effect of the aircraft in disrupting the U-Boat actions when in May 1943 the battle of the Atlantic reached a bloody peak. The U-Boats had shown themselves capable of regularly sinking 500,000 tons of shipping per month in the Atlantic but in May 1943, despite a huge effort, they sank just 212,000 tons. In return they lost 41 U-Boats.[7]

The Germans analysed the causes of their losses and found that 55 per cent were due to aircraft; approximately 20 per cent were possibly due to air attack and 25 per cent through surface attack.[8]

The losses, and the analysis, lead to a temporary withdrawal of the U-Boat force from the North Atlantic. A secret order issued to U-Boat commanders in 24th May stated: "In the last few months our serious U-Boat losses can be mainly ascribed to the superiority of enemy radar equipment which enables him to surprise our boats from the air."

Future operations by the U-Boats were directed to areas less threatened by the Allied Air Forces. Although the battle continued until the war's end, the number of U-Boats in the North Atlantic reached its peak in May 1943. It is difficult to briefly summarise a situation as complex and ever changing as the Battle of the Atlantic, but it was clear from this one event the effect the Sunderlands and other aircraft of Coastal Command were having.

Not that the Allied forces had air superiority over their patrol areas. The German Luftwaffe had directed a long range fighter squadron equipped with the twin engined Ju88 aircraft to search out Coastal Command aircraft over the Bay of Biscay.

In a very active tour of duty F/O Gerrard and his crew onboard DP177 found themselves up against eight of these Ju88s. It was during an anti submarine patrol on 8th August that they spotted the flock of fighters, six of which launched an attack.[9]

The Ju88s split their attacks to try and dilute the effectiveness of the defensive fire. Three fighters were spotted astern and three on the starboard quarter, while a further two well astern held back and did not attack.

As F/O Gerrard jettisoned depth charges, the three fighters astern attacked with cannon from long range and passed by the port side as the Sunderland took evasive action. A single aircraft came in from the starboard bow firing from 600 yards before breaking away, followed by two similar attacks from the port bow, during which the top of the port wing and float were hit. The battle lasted seven minutes before the Ju88s broke away and disappeared. Having escaped with comparatively minor damage Gerrard continued the patrol before returning to base.

The fighters had demonstrated their regard for the defensive capabilities of the Sunderland, of which much had been made.

When it was issued to the RAF the Sunderland was very well defended, compared to other pre-war types. It was equipped with front and rear gun turrets and initially twin hatches for gunners, although the MkIII Sunderlands, such as those built at Windermere, had a mid

6   423 Squadron RCAF Operations Record Book, 1943-1945 Air 27/1833 The National Archives.

7   Saunders, Hilary St George, 1953 (Third impression 1993). The Royal Air Force 1939-1945 Volume 3, The Fight is Won, HMSO 0-11-772114 X

8   Hessler, Gunter, 1989, The U-Boat War in the Atlantic 1939-1945, HMSO 0-11-772603-6

9   10 Squadron RAAF Operations Record Book, 1943 Air 27/152 The National Archives.

upper turret fitted instead. Weak spots were under the wings but they were subsequently protected by additional machine guns fitted to the galley windows.

It appears that the attack of 8th August 1943 was not the only one Gerrard and DP177 had to face. Three days later the same crew and DP177 were lost on patrol. Another Sunderland from 10 Squadron RAAF saw the aircraft but nothing further was heard and all 12 crew were presumed lost.[10] Recent research has shown that a Sunderland was shot down that day by the Ju88s from V/KG 40 - it seems almost certain that this was DP177.[11]

The main duty for the Sunderland over the Atlantic was protection of the transatlantic convoys bringing food and materials to Britain, as well as troops and weapons from the USA to aid the war effort. One of the more unusual convoy attacks was launched by a squadron of German aircraft using radio controlled glider bombs in the Bay of Biscay.

Convoy SL139/MKS30 was a mixed convoy of traffic from both West Africa and Gibraltar to Britain containing 67 merchant vessels, which had already fended off attacks from three separate groups of U-Boats.[12]

On the morning of 21st November 1943, 25 Heinkel He177s attacked. Sunderland DP191 arrived on the scene at 4.16pm and the crew found seven aircraft with at least one German Fw200 Condor also present.[13] The aircraft were seen bombing the convoy and one vessel was obviously hit and smoking. The crew did their best to harry the enemy aircraft and prevent them from getting into attack positions.

On The Water: DP191 with 423 Sqn RCAF on the water at Lough Erne, N Ireland in early 1944.

Jim Wright

10 10 Squadron RAAF Operations Record Book, ibid

11 Goss, Chris, 1997. Bloody Biscay, The History of V Gruppe/Kampfgeschwader 40. Crecy Publishing Ltd. 0-947554-87-4

12 Hessler, Gunter, 1989, The U-Boat War in the Atlantic 1939-1945, HMSO 0-11-772603-6

13 423 Squadron RCAF Operations Record Book, 1943-1945 Air 27/1833 The National Archives.

Sunderland Captain P/O Mike Pearson recalled: "We came across a navy ship and it signalled to us that there was an enemy aircraft in the vicinity. We saw a Liberator go by in front of us being chased by an Fw200. A short time later the sky was full of smoke puffs from the flak that the convoy was putting up.

"As we approached they kept away from us. I remember going into cloud and trying to head them off. We also tried to keep track of them with radar and intercept them that way."[14]

The Sunderland did not directly engage the Germans and was recalled to base after an hour and a half over the convoy. A progress report from 423 Squadron to their headquarters at RCAF Ottawa said: "The aircraft in the circumstances, could not protect the convoy and the crew would be unnecessarily exposed."

DP191 was not the only aircraft patrolling over the convoy. Sunderland O from 201 Squadron also encountered He177s earlier in the day.[15] The Sunderland got close enough to fire at, and claim hits on, an He177 and a Fw200, both of which had been seen to drop glider bombs on the convoy.

Two Liberators from 224 Squadron were sent out. K/224 was in the area from 4.30 until 5.45pm and was involved in four combats with the He177s and was probably the Liberator seen by DP191's crew.

Flying Boat Base:
Pembroke Dock was
the RAF's largest
flying boat base.
The dockyard is
in the foreground
with the town beyond.
The two large hangars
are camouflaged as
rows of houses.

John Evans

14 423 Squadron RCAF Operations Record Book, ibid

15 201Squadron RCAF Operations Record Book, 1944-1945 Air 27/1179 The National Archives.

There is an error in the squadron Operational Record Book which records the Sunderland involved as "W6007" - an aircraft the crew of DP191 had flown a month earlier - but crew member Jim Wright's log book confirms it was actually DP191 used on the day.

Although they had withdrawn in May, the U-Boats were a threat right to the end of the war and Coastal Command crews were kept fully occupied on patrols.

Sunderland captain F/Lt Les Baveystock was one of a small handful of Sunderland pilots to be credited with two U-Boat kills - his second while flying EJ150 for 201 Squadron, also based at Pembroke Dock.

The U-Boat was sighted on 18th August 1944 and surprised Baveystock, who was in the toilet at the time.[16] Pilot F/O MacGregor and the front turret gunner F/Sgt R. Paton simultaneously spotted the wake from a periscope about four miles away on the port bow. F/O Brian Landers, who was in Baveystock's place on the flight deck, ran out the depth charges and sounded the alarm while F/Lt Baveystock ran up the steps to the cockpit, still fastening his trousers.

The crew's diary of the incident states:

"The captain arrived on the bridge. The aircraft circled to port ahead of the periscope feather and the captain took over in the second pilot's seat. An immediate run in was made at 50 feet and six depth charges were dropped. The aircraft tracked over a few yards ahead of the periscope. A straddle was obtained with the entry splashes clearly seen on either side of the periscope."

As soon as the plumes of the explosions had died down a circular eruption of air bubbles was seen from the U-Boat.

Short Break: F/Sgt Jim Wright (Wop/ AG) sitting on the engine of DP191 Lough Erne 1943.

Jim Wright

---

16 Anti-U-boat attacks: reports 1944. ADM 199/522. The National Archives

The diary continues:

"These bubbles with air and froth continued erupting for a further twenty minutes. A few minutes after the attack, oil appeared on the surface gradually increasing to a length of two miles."

Baveystock, already holder of the DFC and DFM, was awarded an immediate DSO for the attack but recorded that: "My second pilot and the crew did it all for me. I was just buttoning up my trousers when I heard the alarm and when I got to the bridge they said `Look, it is a periscope' and I looked and it WAS a periscope. So I just sat in the second pilot's seat and pressed the tit. It was too easy."

The commanding officer of 201 Squadron, Wing Commander K. R. Coates, said: "This one, owing to perfect crew drill, can be quoted as a faultless example of an attack upon a submerged submarine resulting in what would appear to be a well deserved kill. The captain is to be complimented on his crew training and his own skill in bombing from the second pilot's seat."

His comments were echoed by Group Captain G. A. Bolland, station commander at Pembroke Dock, who noted that the best attacks were often made by crews with between 500 and 800 hours of experience on the Sunderland.

The submarine sunk was U-107, a type IX U-Boat commanded by *Oberleutnant zur See* Fritz. An experienced commander, he was in charge of a boat with a long and distinguished history under several commanders. A longer range U-Boat, U-107 had been credited with 38 ships.[17]

Other Windermere-built Sunderlands were involved in successful attacks on U-Boats. On 21st May 1944 the type VIIc U-Boat U-995 survived an attack by DP197, despite being damaged.[18]

DP197 was operating with the training squadron 4(C)OTU based at Alness when on 21st May 1944, under the command of P/O E. T. King, the U-Boat was seen surfacing. The Sunderland crew dropped six depth charges which so damaged U-995 that her

Surface Debris: The only signs that U-107 had been sunk were air bubbling to the surface and bringing with it U-boat charts and and oil slick - later identified by a Royal Navy vessel.

201 Squadron RAF

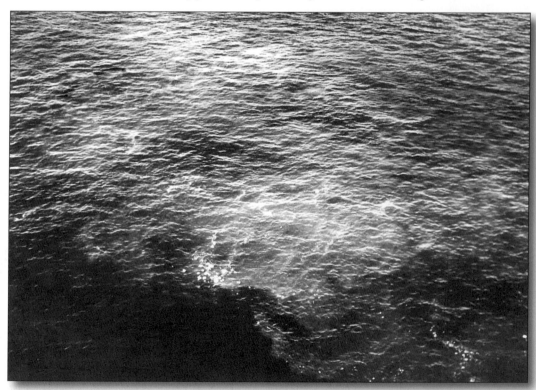

17 Wynn, Kenneth, 1997. U-Boat Operations of World War II Volume I: Career histories, U1-U510. Caxton Editions. 1-84067-525-X

18 .4 (Coastal) Operation Training Unit and Detachment, Operations Record Book, 1944-1946 Air 29/610 The National Archives.

Sub Hunter: EJ150 with 201 Squadron was the aircraft piloted by F/Lt Les Baveystock when he sank U-107.

Ill-Fated Boat: U-107 setting out on patrol. It was to be sunk by F/lt Les Baveystock flying EJ150.

U-boat Memorial: U-995, which was damaged by the crew of DP197, is today on display at Laboe near Keil as a museum boat.

Horst Bredow, U-boat arhive

commander, *Kapitanleutnant* Walter Kohntopp, had to order her back to port. Five crewmen were injured in the attack.

U-995 was unusual in surviving the war and was refitted by the Norwegian navy post war as the KNM *Kaura* between 1952 and 1962.[19] She was later returned to the German Navy and restored to her original U-Boat configuration. Since 1972 she has been on display at Laboe near Keil as a memorial to the U-Boat crews of World War II and is still there today, open to the public.

While operating with 461 Squadron RAAF from Pembroke Dock on 13 August 1944, EJ154 attacked a U-Boat despite heavy flak from the submarine.[20] The crew had used flares to fully illuminate the U-Boat as she recharged her batteries on the surface at 5.35am.

The depth charges straddled the conning tower and silenced the flak. The Sunderland called in escort vessels to the scene, who recovered some debris. When dawn came up one and a half hours after the attack, a large patch of oil was seen 500 yards by 30 yards which was running across the wind lanes on the sea's surface, indicating that it was laid by a moving object.

Wing Commander J. M. Hampshire, in charge of 461 Squadron, praised the crew. "It was a particularly courageous and determined attack by the captain in the face of intense flak. Excellent crew drill and bombing results would appear to have caused at least serious damage to the U-Boat."

The aircraft of Coastal Command frequently worked closely with the Royal Navy's surface vessels, directing them to assist with attacks. On 8th August 1944 DP200, also operating with the Australian 461 Squadron, homed onto a radar contact from three and a half

---

19 Sharpe, Peter, 1998. U-Boat fact File. Midland Publishing Ltd. 1-85780-072-9

20 461 Squadron RAAF Operations Record Book, 1944-1945 Air 27/1914 The National Archives.

miles away shortly before midnight.[21] The crew dropped flares and saw a U-Boat diving. They passed details of the contact onto a navy destroyer which took up the hunt.

The Navy had the benefit of Asdic, a sonar detection system which helped with finding submarines. By the end of the war the technology was made available for the Sunderlands in the form of sonar buoys. "High tea" was the code name for the recently developed sonobuoy that listened underwater for U-Boats and sent information by radio back to the aircraft. On 6th March 1945 EJ151 made contact and spotted an oil slick a mile long.[22] They dropped a "high tea" pattern of buoys which detected a submarine and surface vessels made an attack. When the buoys lost contact the Sunderland returned to base leaving the hunt to the Royal Navy.

Lake Indawgyi: Loading the injured and ill Chindits of 111th Brigade onto the rescue Sunderland deep behind enemy lines.
W/Cdr Dundas Bednall via John Evans

The anti-submarine patrols continued even beyond VE day on 8 May 1945. The news of the surrender only reached the U-Boats when they contacted their base. EJ158 - the last Windermere Sunderland - was on patrol on 19th May 1945 when a fully surfaced U-Boat was seen, following instructions from U-Boat command to fly a blue surrender flag.[23] It was heading due north and was told to halt and wait for a Royal Navy ship to arrive and escort her to a British port.

For both the Sunderland and U-Boat crews the Battle of the Atlantic was finally over.

The Atlantic was not the only battle the Sunderlands were used in - they fought in many theatres including the Mediterranean, South Atlantic and Indian Ocean and Australia. The Windermere Sunderlands were represented around the world.

The ferry flights themselves were sometimes epic operations. When DP189 was assigned to 230 Squadron a route had to be planned to reach the east African Coast from where it could operate over the Indian Ocean, but avoiding enemy and neutral territory.

A crew led by captain A. S. Pedley collected the aircraft from 57 Maintenance Unit at Wig Bay in September 1943.[24] The first leg was to Gibraltar, a well proven route across the Bay of Biscay avoiding neutral Spain and Portugal and ever mindful of the long range German fighters. Rather than the more obvious route through the Mediterranean, the crew continued south down the west coast of Africa, using bases set up by other RAF squadrons to protect the south Atlantic convoy routes. The "scenic route" as Don Holloway remembered it, then took them straight across the centre of the continent to Mombassa and Dar-es-Salaam ready for active operations.

The squadron flew operations covering much of the region from East Africa, India, Ceylon and the Maldive Islands. DP189 had a relatively uneventful career on its warm water operations apart from one accident when the keel was damaged at Kegli Island

21 461 Squadron RAAF Operations Record Book, ibid

22 422 Squadron RCAF Operations Record Book, 1942-1945 Air 27/1831 The National Archives.

23 422 Squadron RCAF Operations Record Book, ibid

24 230 Squadron Operations Record Book, 1943-1945 Air 27/1423 The National Archives.

Operation River: Back in the Brahamaputra, the wounded are ferried to the shore on a DUKW. The two Sunderlands used on the operation were nicknamed Gert and Daisy, after radio characters of the time.

Imperial War Museum

base.[25] In April 1944 intelligence considered there were only two U-Boats in 222 Group's area which controlled 230 Squadron.[26]

However, in May 1944 230 Squadron were tasked with a unique operation for which only flying boats were capable, and DP180, O for Orange, was given the job.

Deep in the Burma jungle the Chindits had been involved in intense fighting behind Japanese lines, but needed resupply from the air and evacuation of wounded and sick. The terrain and monsoon conditions had made land airstrips unusable, so the group were ordered to make for Lake Indawgyi to wait for a Sunderland.

Operation River[27] started on 27th May when DP180 left Koggala for Calcutta and then flew on to Dibrugarh on the River Brahamaputra, which was to be the forward base for operations. From there, close to the eastern range of the Himalayas, the Sunderland would fly due east, over 12,000 feet high mountains into enemy held territory.

Led by Squadron Leader J. L. Middleton, the detachment made their first attempt to reach Lake Indawgyi on 1st June but were forced back by appalling weather conditions, with solid cloud cover from 500 feet to 20,000 feet.

Navigator on the second Sunderland to take part in the mission (JM659), F/O A. J. Norton, explained that it was not the place to be in Sunderlands with Bristol Pegasus

25 Roberts, Nicholas, 1977. Aircraft Crash log number 3: Short Sunderland. Private.

26 230 Squadron Operations Record Book, 1943-1945 Air 27/1423 The National Archives.

27 230 Squadron Operations Record Book appendices, 1941-1945 Air 27/1425 The National Archives.

engines that had been reconditioned in the Far East. The engines had a life span of only about 60 hours and the ceiling limit for the Sunderland was about 14,000 feet giving, at best, marginal clearance above the mountains. More worryingly F/O Norton and the navigator on DP180, F/O Noel Verney, both felt the spot heights for mountain tops shown on their maps were suspect.

The weather conditions also caused difficulties on the Bramaputra which was full and fast flowing. On occasions the Sunderlands had to be towed to their moorings by American amphibious DUKWs that battled against ten knot currents.

The second attempt by DP180 to reach the lake was more successful, despite continuing bad weather and the lack of a fighter escort, which disliked the weather even more than the Sunderland crews. The Sunderland landed at the north end of the lake at 2.20 pm and loaded 32 casualties on board who had been rowed out to them on dinghies. Airborne within the hour, the return journey was made without incident. The lake had proved large, deep and free from surface hazards, which made take offs and landings comparatively easy.

The load carried on that first trip was experimental because of the steep climb needed to clear the mountains. On the next three days the load was gradually increased each day from 36 to 39 and then 41 casualties. The P-51 Mustang fighter force even managed to battle through the clouds to make their rendezvous. Their presence was appreciated on 5th June when on both the outward and return journeys eight enemy fighters, possibly Zeros, were seen, although the clouds gave sufficient cover.

DP180 made its final sortie of the first phase of the operation on 9th June when the fighter escort was forced to turn back because of the appalling weather. The Sunderland battled on through the weather and landed on the lake at 8am collecting another 41 casualties.

The squadron operational record book[28] records that a total of 269 casualties had been evacuated. The intelligence officer recorded "Although the flying conditions were extremely bad during the whole course of the operation, imposing a severe strain on the crew, everybody felt gratified that a useful job of work had been successfully accomplished."

The operation attracted the attention of a large number of high-ranking officers, not least Air Marshall Sir John Baldwin, commander of the 3rd Tactical Air Force who visited Dibrugarh to see the progress of Operation River for himself.

While DP180 was prepared to return to base, the second Sunderland, JM659 "Q", took over and arrived at Dibrugarh on 6th June. The following day two sorties were made with S/Ldr Middleton on board while DP180 underwent maintenance.

Bad weather continued to hinder the operations but worse still, on 20th June a DUKW collided with Q's wing float. The mainspar and struts were damaged beyond repair and the float had to be removed while new parts were brought in. While waiting for the parts to arrive, on July 4th, a strong wind caught the aircraft and sent the port wing deep into the water, flooding the whole aircraft.

DP180 had to take over the next mission to Lake Indawgyi on 30th June, in characteristic heavy rain. They delivered an assault boat to the ground troops and collected 40 casualties.

The inbound flights continued to drop supplies, coined currency and even some additional personnel, while full loads of casualties were recovered - and on one occasion even a disconsolate-looking Japanese prisoner.

On 3rd July, after setting off early for the lake, the crew heard that the lake had been strafed by a Japanese fighter just 20 minutes after they had left, when they would normally have still been loading the aircraft. It was the last flight made into Burma, the next day the operation finished and DP180 left for Calcutta carrying Wing Commander Drake AFC and public relations personnel, who were keen to highlight just how successful Operation River had been. They also ferried back the crew from JM659.

---

28 230 Squadron Operations Record Book appendices. ibid

F/O Norton's most vivid recollection of the mission had been the condition of the evacuees. They were all in a terrible physical condition suffering from battle wounds, malaria, typhus, pneumonia and dysentery, and all in an exhausted state. Although given good care afterwards, the survival rate was not thought to be high.

After the final flight the Chindits tried their own overland evacuation by loading casualties into boats and making an arduous trip down river to friendly territory.

The mission had undoubtedly been a success in demonstrating the flexibility of the Sunderland and in evacuating a total of 537 casualties. Mountbatten himself had supported the use of flying boats and publicity even gave the two Sunderlands new names: Gert and Daisy, after the famous radio characters created by Elsie and Doris Waters.

Immediate awards were made to the crew of DP180. The DFC was awarded to S/Ldr Middleton, the captain F/Lt Jack Rand, and navigator F/O Noel Verney. The DFM was awarded to flight engineer F/Sgt R. Webber.

Another warm water posting for the Sunderlands units was along the West Africa coasts, protecting the convoys between Britain and the Far East. The RAF had several bases along the West African coast. Freetown in Sierra Leone was the headquarters of the commander in chief of the South Atlantic and was used as a base for the flying boats. Donitz had recognised the importance of the port for shipping along the coast and sent long range U-Boats to the area, forcing a response from the Allies.

The RAF presence included 95, 204 and 270 Squadrons, as well as the French manned 343 Squadron - six of the Windermere Sunderlands served in these units. Most of the patrols were convoy escort duties. DP186 provided cover for convoy SL139 on 8th November 1943, the convoy later attacked by German aircraft with glider bombs in the Bay of Biscay.[29]

None of the Windermere aircraft in this theatre were involved in attacks on U-Boats, the numbers off the West African coast being far less than in the north Atlantic. But nevertheless the patrols were kept up.

Occasionally they were called on to undertake rescue duties. DP194 was used in a search for a missing French Wellington bomber from 344 Squadron on 28th August 1944. Nothing was found despite searches by several aircraft.[30]

Just afloat:
Antipodean Wreck
- A26-6, the former
DP192 is towed to
the harbour by a tug.
Vic Hodgkinson

29 95 Squadron Operations Record Book, 1941-1943 Air 27/761 The National Archives.

30 95 Squadron Operations Record Book, 1944-1945 Air 27/762 The National Archives.

Antipodean Wreck - A26-6, the former DP192 was written off after a collision. The nose caved in after the pilot collided with a Dolphin - a telegraph pole sized timber marker used to indicate the safe channel to the harbour entrance. The aircraft sank up to the wing level.

Vic Hodgkinson

The crew on DP186 found themselves searching for colleagues when another aircraft from their squadron went missing. Sunderland D/95 (W6076) was reported missing on 13th December 1944.[31] After patrolling along the coast they found the Sunderland on the water at Dakar suffering from engine trouble. They landed alongside and both returned to base the same day.

The only recorded loss among the six Sunderlands was DP182 when operating with 343 Squadron.

Originally with 204 Squadron in March 1943, DP182 was transferred to the French squadron during May 1943, part of the first batch of three Sunderlands to join the squadron. The aircraft was lost on a patrol on 2nd February 1944. It suffered engine failure and was ditched in the Atlantic, although the crew were later rescued.[32]

The farthest service from their country of origin was when a group of six Sunderlands, including DP192,[33] was sent across the globe for the Australian government. The RAAF operated their well-known 10 Squadron from the UK but also equipped a squadron with Sunderlands for operations in their home waters.

The unit, 40 Squadron RAAF, was formed under the command of Vic Hodgkinson initially at Townsville and then moved to a permanent base at Port Moresby. The six Sunderlands with the squadron were stripped of military equipment and used for transport duties from March 1943 until the end of the war, when the five surviving aircraft were sold to Trans Oceanic Airways which converted three to passenger carrying duties.

The Sunderlands carried up to 40 troops and 10,000 lbs of mail a day to Townsville and a weekly run with stores to Darwin.

DP192 was the only one of the squadron's aircraft to be lost in an accident. On the day it was being piloted by F/Lt Williams who had served in the Australian squadrons and been under an attack by Ju88s over the Bay of Biscay. Both his health and confidence in his flying had suffered afterwards and Vic Hodgkinson had recommended his posting off flying duties, although no action was taken by headquarters.

On landing at Townsville he had kept DP192 on the step, taxying at speed towards the narrow harbour entrance. The channel into the harbour was marked by "Dolphins",

---

31 95 Squadron Operations Record Book, 1944-1945 ibid

32 Bowyer, Chaz, 1989. The Short Sunderland, Aston publications. 0 7110 0665 2

33 A M Form 78, Aircraft movement card for DP192, RAF Museum.

wooden pylons of about three feet in diameter set into the sea bed. He collided head-on with one and immediately the aircraft sank. The troops and crew managed to abandon the aircraft safely and the nearly empty fuel tanks gave some buoyancy, keeping the wings just on the surface.

A rescue tug was sent to tow the aircraft back to harbour and in the process caused considerable damage to the tail and main planes. The aircraft was dragged ashore, beyond hope of repair, and was broken up on the spot by an RAAF salvage crew. F/Lt Williams received his posting from the squadron with no action taken against him.

Several others of the Windermere Sunderlands met their ends as a result of accidents, a tragic consequence of operating aircraft close to their limits during wartime.

Five crew on board DP181 were killed in a landing accident at Castle Archdale on Lough Erne in rough conditions on 11th November 1943.[34] The aircraft bounced on landing and the heavy landing which resulted caused the bow to split open. Still heavily laden, the incoming water caused the aircraft to sink very quickly. The pilot, F/Lt M. D. Lee was injured in the crash but four died on board and one later from injuries. The court of inquiry found that the airfield had failed to inform the pilot of the sea state, although it also added that he should have been prepared for a rough sea landing.

DP181 did not stay on the bottom of the lough for long. The RAF had commissioned a local salvage firm to recover aircraft. On 21st November DP181 was beached at Castle Archdale and the remaining bodies of the crew recovered.

The first Windermere built Sunderland, DP176, met her end out in the Atlantic when one of the MkIII's weaknesses proved to be her downfall. The Bristol Pegasus engine was overworked on an operational Sunderland, being run at high power ratings for most of the time. In a reconditioned engine the biggest weakness was in the propeller reduction gear. A failure meant a propeller would fly off without warning - an event which happened to several startled crews, and all the worse if the propeller hit the neighbouring engine. A MkIII Sunderland with more than one engine out was all but impossible to keep flying.

At 2am on 15th April 1943 DP176 was returning to base when the propeller on the outer engine flew off without warning, hitting the inner.[35] The aircraft was at a height of 4,000 feet and an SOS was hurriedly transmitted. Only a minute later the pilot, F/Lt J. V. Gibson, ditched the aircraft. The port side float was lost and the wing tip dug in. The Sunderland tipped onto its nose and remained in that position for about ten minutes with the water level with the mid upper turret. The squadron operational record books records the incident:

"All members of the crew left the aircraft within 20 seconds of ditching. Only two dinghies were got out. One was floated towards three members of the crew who were clinging to the aerial but it floated away unopened with the current and they did not get to it. Two of these three reached the other dinghy. The remaining one, F/O Waters (Navigator) who was being assisted over to the dinghy, broke away and disappeared below the water and was not seen again. The remainder of the crew got into the dinghy, except F/Lt. Davies (Tail Gunner) and Sgt. Galloway (Flight Engineer) who were not seen after they left the aircraft. At 08.05 Sunderland "O" arrived and remained with the dinghy. About 12.00 Catalina "L" arrived and both aircraft remained in company. At 12.35 Sunderland sent signal "Ship approaching now" and left vicinity. At 15.10 hours Destroyer (L86) Wensleydale arrived and picked up all survivors."

The surviving crew were later landed at Devonport.

34 423 Squadron RCAF Operations Record Book, 1943-1945 Air 27/1833 The National Archives.

35 119 Squadron Operations Record Book, 1910-1980 Air 27/910 The National Archives.

Sunderland EJ155 v U-boat U-387

Windermere built Sunderland EJ155 was operational with 330 (Norwegian) Squadron at Sullom Voe in the Shetlands. On the night on 19th July 1944 the aircraft encountered U-387 off the Norwegian coast. The following record of 24 hours in the North Sea is taken from 330 Squadron's Operational Record Book and U-387's logbook.

The Captain of the U-boat was Rudolf Büchler whose mission was to attack the arctic convoys. On the Sunderland, Captain Lt. B. Th-Nielsen's mission was to stop him.

EJ155	U-387
19th July 17.44 hours First operation sortie - took off from base on anti-submarine patrol	19th July 17.00 Incoming wireless message Captain Büchler ordered to sail back to Vestfjord AF2383 No unnecessary attacks to be launched. After air attacks details immediately details about types of aeroplanes and result of defence to be reported immediately.
23.10 Radar Contact bearing 18 miles. Investigated	Irregular clicks in radar detecting equipment, possible aircraft in vicinity
23.20 From 800 feet up at three and a half miles away sighted a fully surfaced U-Boat. Aircraft turned to port to take advantage of cloud cover to avoid detection and approached up track of the U-Boat. Broke cloud cover at 600 feet three quarters of a mile from the U-Boat	Büchler decided to go up on deck
and dived to attack from the port beam of the submarine	On the way heard the cry "Aircraft!" and immediately hit by heavy depth charges and hit by gunfire
Estimated good straddle just aft of the conning tower Two depth charges on the port side and four on the starboard side. Tail gunner saw the points of entry	One depth charge hits the upper deck edge and falls in the water. Direct hit by a Sunderland approached diagonally from port out of the deep hanging cloud cover from nearby
All depth charges appeared to envelope the U-Boat in one big plume	Our own weapons hardly had chance to be brought to bear and the 3.7cm fails (fastener wedge jammed fast) below decks all is in a muddle and confusion, especially in the central and front part of the ship. Lights are out
U-Boat turned 180 degrees to starboard and opened up flak forcing the aircraft to take evasive action. When first seen the U-Boat was very high out of water. After it was still on an even keel but the decks were almost awash	The order to abandon ship was given but immediately recalled as the boat still afloat
Six minutes later the contact disappeared and radar contact was lost	Transmitter still clear, short signal but not communicated. No further attack. Plane keeps going into the distance and disappears at times into the clouds
The marine marker was seen to disappear and was lost in heavy rain squalls.	After about 15 minutes the state under the decks can be assessed, the boat can be reported clear for diving
Subsequent markers were also lost. Heavy rain and low cloud prevented the crew from seeing if any wreckage or oil patches were in the vicinity.	Plane is particularly far away. Boat is watertight to the crack in a weld seam in the pressure hull over pipe one. Water forcing its way in not considerable. Battery 2 badly damaged. Several cells cracked. Flooding moving slowly towards the battery room
After the U-Boat had turned to starboard it was hardly moving. The first depth charge was estimated as having dropped 100 feet from the port side of the submarine	

EJ155	U-387
23.50 Radioed to command that attacked U-boat. Estimated two hits. Last seen in position 68029' N 07019'E. Searched failed to find U-boat or wreckage	Under water. There are numerous failures in all installations *Matr Gefr* Scholtys has a splinter graze in foot through shot in arm *Matr Ob Gefr* [Seaman 1st Class] Hess grazing shot in nose
02.00 Off patrol	Only cleared for limited diving because of damage. especially to weapons and pressure hull Further attacks fail to develop. Carry on underwater toward Lofoten
0700 Landed back at base	16.26 Repairs good enough to allow us to surface Balancing pressure took six minutes because of faulty barometer which resulted in nausea and vomiting in several sailors. Pumps working slowly 12 cells of battery two have leaked and not enough bridging rails to bypass them all. The empty cells smoke heavily
	17.00 Land in sight Port side electric motor is running warm even so still using both electric motors to maintain 7 to10 knots

U-387 finally entered Narvik at 16.30 on 22nd July - three days after the attack. Three days later, with temporary repairs done, the submarine put to sea again to transfer from Narvik to Trondheim. At 18.30 on 26th July U-387 arrived at the safety of the Trondheim U-boat pens and was made fast inside the dockyard.

The U-boat was repaired and went back out on patrol. On 9th December 1944 she was sunk by HMS *Bamburgh* Castle and all 51 crew on board were lost.

Lucky Crew:
The crew of U-387
who narrowly escaped
being sunk by the crew
of EJ155.

Horst Bredow,
U-boat arhive

Sunderlands at peace

Even before the war had ended plans were being made for peacetime air transport. Short Brothers had developed the Sunderland in parallel with their famous "C-Class" Empire flying boat, which crossed the globe carrying passengers and mail in luxurious conditions in the 1930s, and saw uses for Sunderlands converted to take passengers.

As early as 1943 the Government had advanced plans for commercial aircraft service post war, although at that time they had not included flying boats. This prompted Short Brothers' partner in the Shetland, Saunders Roe, to produce a detailed study on the future for flying boats in commercial service. The report, which looked at potential routes and designs of docks, argued that, at larger sizes, the flying boat had an advantage over landplanes.[1]

While plans were being drawn up for making the Shetland into a passenger aircraft, Short Brothers also came up with ways to make the long serving Sunderland into an attractive airliner.

During hostilities some Sunderlands were converted to carry passengers for BOAC, replacing Empire flying boats. These Short Hythes, named after the passenger terminal on the Solent, were austerity conversions with the military equipment removed and rudimentary bench seating installed. The first conversions entered service in 1943.[2]

After VE day Short Brothers came up with a plan to streamline the Sunderland hull with a reprofiled nose and tail, roughly based on the shape of the Empire boats. Converted Sunderlands were renamed Sandringhams and produced in a range of standards for several airlines.

Uruguayan Airliner: CX-AKR ex DP195 built for CAUSA being launched down the slip at Belfast. This is a Sunderland civil conversion without the full Sandringham nose and tail.

Bombardier via Ron Parsons

1   The Case for the Flying Boat, 25th Nov 1943 Flight, No1822, Vol XLIV,
2   Barnes, C H, 1967. Shorts Aircraft since 1900, Putnam.

It is noticeable that several of the aircraft repaired at the Windermere CRO works were chosen. Clearly the better condition aircraft were being selected. The first commercial order came from the South American airline *Compania Argentina de Aeronavegacion Dodero*, Buenos Aires, owned by Argentinean shipping magnate Senor Dodero.[3] DD834, which had been repaired in Windermere in April 1944, was converted and initially given the UK civilian registration G-AGPZ and named Argentina. The conversion included Pratt and Whitney engines and was designated Sandringham 2, the earlier prototype being Sandringham 1.

The Dodero aircraft were built to a very high standard but when an airline in neighbouring Uruguay, *Compania Aeronautica Uruguaya* S. A. - CAUSA, wanted up to five similar flying boats they chose a simpler, and cheaper, standard. They would operate along the Rio del Plata between Montevideo and Buenos Aires.

One of the two aircraft was built at Windermere and was part of a batch of 24 Mk III Sunderlands declared as surplus by the Air Ministry. Of these 12 were in the UK and instructions were given for two, recently off the production line, to be selected.

"It is important that the machines finally chosen should be a credit to the British aircraft industry," stated a memo within the Ministry of Aircraft production.[4]

It was to be the start of saga of arguments, political wrangling and mistakes which eventually cost the Air Ministry dear.

The Ministry wanted to charge £15,000 each for the Sunderlands, excluding any reconditioning carried out by Short Brothers which was estimated at between £6,500 and £12,300. Short Brothers drew up a cheap scheme for Causa which did not involve the new tail and nose sections of a true Sandringham. This civil Sunderland conversion to carry 40 passengers would cost £9,000.

Civil Sunderland: G-AGWW was built for CAUSA from the military EJ156. Seen taking off from Belfast Lough in May 1946.

Bombardier via Ron Parsons

3   Barnes, C H, ibid

4   Sale of Sunderland Flying Boats to Short Brothers for Supply to CAUSA of Uruguay. AVIA 15/2451. The National Archives.

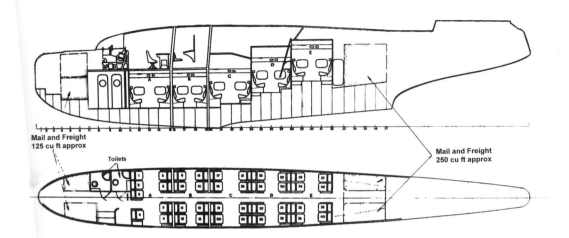

Forty Seater: A Sunderland converted into a Sandringham has a two deck layout. But the cheaper conversion for Causa had 40 seats in five compartments on a single deck.

National Archives

On 12th June 1945 Causa were told the aircraft would cost £27,500 plus £800 for spare engines and £200 for spare propellers and they ordered two, with an option for a third.

Shorts had some difficulties fulfilling their order due to a strike at their Belfast works. Causa also caused their own disruptions by suddenly deciding they wanted Bristol Pegasus 38 engines which had fully feathering propellers rather than the RAF standard Pegasus XVIII.

The problems were made worse in October when Dodero started to fight to block the sale to Causa. He was convinced they would transfer the aircraft to his Argentine rival Sud America who were on a black list of companies. While the arguments raged, the first Causa aircraft, EJ156, had arrived at Belfast ready for work to start. The second aircraft ML876 arrived shortly afterwards.

The aircraft were finally fitted out and test flown from Poole in March 1946. EJ156 went to Causa as expected but the second aircraft did indeed go to Sud America. Dodero then bought ML876 from them and fitted his own Pratt and Whitney Twin Wasp engines.

A year later the Ministry were still seeking payment, which finally arrived although Shorts Brothers had made a loss on the deal. Because Dodero had got the second civil Sunderland he had let Causa have the spare engines and propellers which he did not need and had deprived Shorts of the spares business. The two aircraft had been sold to Causa for £27,900 each but Short Brothers had spent £41,263 on the conversions, £6,800 on engines and £2,360 on propellers. . Including the cost of the aircraft, the deficit on the deal had been £28,823 - more than the cost of another aircraft.

Within the Ministry of Supply, which had taken over the role of the Ministry of Aircraft Production, it was decided to simply "call it a day."

"After all we have got rid of some surplus aircraft and engines. We found Shorts some valuable work at an opportune moment and we did a handsome job for an influential customer in a most important market," was the conclusion reached in the ministry.[5]

They may have been right since it was not the last order Short Brothers received from South America. Several other Sandringhams and civil Sunderlands were to be sold to Dodero and to *Aerolineas Argentinas*, which absorbed Dodero's fleet in 1949. Windermere-built DP195, another civil Sunderland conversion, was sold to Causa, given the Uruguayan registration CX-AKR and named *Capitan Bosio Lanza*. The South American flying boats continued a long service until, in January 1967, the last six were finally broken up for scrap. [6]

5   Sale of Sunderland Flying Boats to Short Brothers for Supply to CAUSA of Uruguay. AVIA 15/2451. National Archives.

6   Barnes, C H, 1967. Shorts Aircraft since 1900, Putnam.

The Ploughman. EJ153 hit high ground while on a night exercise but managed to fly off. It took the help of several pumps and boats to gradually bring the aircraft ashore.

S/Ldr E W Beer RAF (rtd)

Before filling in the holes with cement so the aircraft could be flown to Belfast for repairs, the station commander ordered all the in flight shoring to be put back and the hull filled with water to show how effective the emergency repairs had been. The water pouring from the colander like hull demonstrated his point perfectly.

S/Ldr E W Beer RAF (rtd)

The post war demand for military aircraft was, of course, considerably less than during the war and many surplus aircraft were scrapped or simply dumped. The RAF greatly increased the number of Sunderlands in store at 57MU's site at Wig Bay. It was from this pool that aircraft for civil conversion or squadron service were drawn.

In the UK two Sunderland squadrons and a training unit continued operating until the late 1950s. 201 and 230 Squadrons were both based at Pembroke Dock in the 1950s while the training unit, 235 OCU, was at the old flying boat base at Calshot, near Southampton.

The unit ran 16 week courses to train Sunderland crews, on flights of up to six or seven hours. The training schedule was hard on the aircraft with a large number of landings made - occasionally heavy landings. Major hull repairs had to be carried out on several of the unit's aircraft.[7]

One aircraft, EJ153, needed its hull repaired but the cause was far from routine. The aircraft was on a night-time low level bombing mission using the Chesil target, above Chesil Beach. The student crew were on the last trip of the course when the aircraft hit the top of the hill. Remarkably the Sunderland slid along the hill top, its hull cutting a massive furrow, and then flew off the far side, still airworthy. On board S/Ldr E W Beer and the rest of his crew spent a busy night shovelling earth out of the aircraft, although it was clear it was not seaworthy. They shored the damage as best they could, flew round until daylight to burn off fuel and prepared for a landing.

When the Sunderland touched down the shoring popped out of place and the pilot beached the aircraft on mudflats to prevent her sinking. Surrounded by marine craft and

London Celebration: DP198, 201-A, moored on the Thames in front of the Tower of London
201 Squadron RAF

7   235 OCU Operations Record Book AIR 29/2170 The National Archives.

with men balanced in the tail to keep the nose up, the Sunderland was eventually dragged up the beach. With the hull plugged with concrete the Sunderland was flown to Belfast for permanent repairs.

The Pembroke Dock based squadrons had a schedule of training missions involving bombing and gunnery practice as well as exercises with naval forces. 1954 provided a unique opportunity for the flying boat pilots to take their aircraft to the high arctic in support of the British North Greenland Expedition.

In May DP200, which had joined 230 Squadron in February 1954, was used for practice in taking aerial photographs for a planned photomosaic of north Greenland. On 31 July the squadron detachment left Pembroke Dock to begin the evacuation of the expedition from their base camp at Britannia Lake - 77 degrees north.[8]

DP200 - Z/230 flew the first stage to Reykjavik and then on to Young Sound. They carried out the photomosaic of a 200 square miles area of Greenland - believed to be the first time a Sunderland had been successfully used on a photographic survey. On the trip the flying of DP200 was shared by the captain F/O Reddish and the commanding officer, Squadron Leader Bennett.

The expedition members and their huskies were successfully recovered and the Sunderlands returned to base on 11th August.

Another major detachment took place the following summer when both DP200 and EJ153 were part of a squadron detachment to the Far East. The RAF had maintained flying boat squadrons based at Hong Kong and Seletar in Singapore after the war. 230 Squadron sent their crews out to Seletar to join in naval exercises.

Four aircraft from the squadron took part in the exercise Anzex One and completed all but one of their 19 sorties. Only one submarine was sighted, by the crew of EJ153, and a kill was claimed after it had been "bombed" with smoke flares. The submarine had been in an area declared a haven and the kill was not counted - especially when it later emerged that it had been a Russian submarine detailed to shadow the exercises.[9]

At the end of 1956 the squadron was told they were to be disbanded. On 30th October EJ153 had flown to Castle Archdale and was taxying down a marked channel ready for take off when the aircraft struck a submerged rock. Bill Campbell, a crew member, recalled how he was on the lower deck at the time.

"I was in the ward room with some NATO personnel when we heard a terrible graunching sound and then my feet started to get wet."

The aircraft was stuck fast on the rock until flotation gear was brought out. The onboard pumps were barely coping but they managed to beach the aircraft. The accident had been caused by an unusually low lough level. After the accident the aircraft was left in the hangar at Castle Archdale, but with the imminent disbandment of UK based flying boat squadrons, the repair work was never carried out.

The use for Sunderlands in the UK might have ended but they were still in demand overseas. One particularly surprising order, as late as 1952, came from the Royal New Zealand Air Force which wanted 16 Mk V Sunderlands to replace its ageing Catalina fleet.

With the Sunderland production line long since closed down, the only available aircraft were those in storage at Wig Bay. Sixteen suitable airframes were chosen including DP191, which had spent eight years at Wig Bay. The Sunderlands were fully rebuilt to the new RNZAF specification and the pilots even joined the course run by 235 OCU at Calshot before ferrying their "new" Sunderlands to Fiji.[10]

DP191 - given the RNZAF serial number NZ4109 - joined 5 Squadron based at Lauthala Bay in Fiji and was used to provide a vital lifeline to many outlying island

8   230 Squadron Operations Record Book AIR 27/2668 The National Archives

9   230 Squadron Operations Record Book AIR 27/2668 The National Archives.

10 235 OCU Operations Record Book AIR 29/2170 The National Archives.

*Disbanding: DP198 forms the backdrop for the final 201 Squadron photo on
31st January 1957 when the squadron disbands as a flying boat unit.*

201 Squadron RAF

communities. Medical supplies, passengers and freight were carried to locations where there was no runway for land planes. In many cases seriously ill patients were evacuated to hospitals in a few hours when a ship would have taken days to arrive. Occasionally 5 Squadron moved to Singapore where they took part in maritime exercises with their RAF counterparts.

In August that year the RNZAF nearly lost one of their Sunderlands when NZ4111 became stuck on an uncharted coral reef at Nukunono. The coral had ripped open the hull but the crew managed to beach the aircraft. Other Sunderlands of the squadron, including NZ4109, flew in salvage equipment. Beaching legs were fitted and NZ4111 was driven up onto the beach where repairs could be carried out. Hull plates were repaired and replaced and on 12th September she was flown out sporting the new name "Nukunono Baby".

In October 1955 a major search operation was mounted for the vessel "Joyita" which had disappeared with 25 passengers and crew on board. The vessel had been sailing from Apia to Fakaofa in the Tokelaus, 270 miles north of Samoa. But she never arrived and on 6th October was declared overdue. NZ4109 began the search the following day and after an all day search landed at Samoa. The aircraft was out again the next day and joined by NZ4108 as the scale of the search built up.

Over the ensuing days over 120,000 square miles of ocean were searched in an effort to find the boat or her passengers, but nothing was seen until the waterlogged hulk of the "Joyita" was spotted on 10th November, with no sign of the 25 on board. The mystery of their disappearance was never solved.

South Pacific Skies: NZ4109 ex DP191 over the South Pacific Ocean with the RNZAF. Note the additional aerials on the RNZAF Sunderlands
RNZAF Museum

Flying postmen: HMS Belfast *seen from DP199 in Alacrity Anchorage off the mouth of the Yangtse after HMS* Amethyst *was trapped by Communist troops. The Sunderland was delivering the mail to keep up the morale on the ship. Alongside* Belfast *are HMS* Black Swan *and* Green Ranger. **Dick Dulieu**

The RNZAF Sunderlands continued to give good service for many years, with some withdrawn from service to provide spares to keep others airworthy. NZ4109 was withdrawn from service in December 1956 and flown to the main base at Hobsonville for long term storage. After parts had been removed to keep the rest of the fleet flying, the remainder of the hulk was sold for scrap in 1967. The last RNZAF Sunderland was withdrawn from Fiji in April 1967. One aircraft was preserved, NZ4115 (formerly RAF SZ584) was presented to the Museum of Transport and Technology at Auckland.

The RAF also maintained their own presence in the Far East from soon after VJ Day. Squadrons moved back to bases they had occupied before the war and 88 Squadron was formed at Kai Tak in Hong Kong, initially as a transport squadron.[11]

In 1946 their main duty was a twice weekly transport run between Kai Tak and Iwakuni in Japan, and from April 1948 the squadron took on more general duties, including exercises with the naval forces in the South China Sea. This was the situation when DP199 was ferried out from the UK in May 1948. Missions included general training for the crews but also some aerial photography, although conflict was soon to return to the region.

In 20th April 1949 the order was given for all the squadron aircraft to be armed. HMS *Amethyst* had been damaged by gunfire in the battle between Chinese communist troops under Mao Tse

Mail for the fleet: Dick Dulieu unloading DP199 on a supply trip to Iwakuni.

Dick Dulieu

11 88 Squadron Operations Record Book AIR 27/2440 The National Archives.

Tung and the nationalist forces under Chiang Kai Shek. The incident created headlines around the world and it was 88 Squadron's Sunderlands which were called in to help. Under heavy artillery fire medical supplies were landed for the warship by Sunderland D/88 - ML772.[12]

DP199 - C/88 - was held in reserve at Kai Tak with others from the squadron and continued bombing and gunnery practice.

HMS *Belfast*, the heavy cruiser now preserved on the Thames in London, was the flagship of the Far East fleet and on 1st May commander in chief, Admiral Maddin called for a mail delivery to the fleet at Alacrity Anchorage off the mouth of the Yangtse River. DP199 piloted by S/Ldr Dick Dulieu landed alongside and received an invitation to go on board *Belfast* to join the admiral for tea. With nowhere to moor the Sunderland the second pilot was left taxiing in circles around the fleet to the amusement of the sailors lining the rails of their ships while the tea party was concluded.

The fighting soon passed HMS *Amethyst* and she made her daring escape down the river, evading the guns of the communist forces, without the need for the main fleet to intervene. But by 14th May the communist troops were closing in on Shanghai and it was announced that all British nationals were to be evacuated.

The Sunderlands of 88 Squadron were in action again and F/88 brought out 26 passengers on the 15th while the next day DP199 brought back 38 British nationals. Other aircraft brought out 57 before Shanghai fell to the communists a few days later.

S/Ldr Fred Weaver had been one of the pilots with 88 Squadron during the evacuation. He recalled how the crews were all roused from their living quarters and told radio contact with Shanghai had been broken. The squadron aircraft had set off during the night at half hourly intervals with strict instructions only to land if they saw a man waving a large green flag and if the previous Sunderland had already left.

Royal Escort:
SS Gothic, *carrying*
the Queen, was
met on 8th April
1954 by a flight of
Sunderlands of 88
Sqn 550 miles west
of Ceylon for a flypast
before providing escort
patrols all the way
back to Ceylon.

   National Archives

12. 88 Squadron Operations Record Book ibid.

"Flying low over the terrain we passed over a number of military looking groups but we had no idea as to whether they might be friend or foe. Then, yes, there was a man on the bank waving a green flag and the previous Sunderland was just getting airborne. We picked up 35 passengers complete with boxes, bags and prams all in a somewhat hasty manner. The whole operation was a brilliant success."

In the months after the evacuation the squadron returned to training duties - a necessary prelude as war clouds loomed over Korea.

DP199 returned to the UK in May 1950 to be replaced with another Sunderland fresh out of major servicing. The aircraft were ferried out via the RAF bases across the Mediterranean, Middle East and Indian Ocean. When EJ155 was issued to 88 Squadron in December 1952, the crew found themselves involved in an epic ferry flight to the squadron's new base at Seletar.

On 20th November the aircraft set out from the UK but failed to make the first stop at Gibraltar after an engine failed. On 1st December they tried again and reached Gibraltar, setting out the next day for Marsaxlokk in Malta - where trouble struck again. During a taxy test number three engine failed and a fire broke out in the carburettor which blew a hole in the collector ring. The engine could not be repaired quickly - the only answer was to have a complete new engine collector ring and exhaust manufactured and shipped out.

It meant the crew got to spend Christmas in Malta - and the New Year. They had arrived on 1st December but it was not until 6th January that their aircraft was ready to fly again.

The next leg to Fanara in Egypt went well and the Sunderland was refuelled ready for the trip to Bahrein. They set off not realising the fuel had been contaminated and they were forced back to Fanara with all four engines coughing - a frightening experience. After fresh fuel was added, the rest of the trip somehow managed to go smoothly as the aircraft was taken to Bahrein, Korangi Creek near Karachi, Trincomalee in Ceylon and on to Seletar.

The whole journey from leaving on 23rd October had taken until 12th January. The crew were immediately sent on ten days leave to recover.[13]

The Sunderlands operating in the Far East had to deal with the Korean War and the Malaysian Emergency as well as the Communist take over of China.

On arrival in Singapore, EJ155's first mission over Malaya was a "Firedog" mission on 18th February 1953. The Sunderland would be loaded with large numbers of small bombs which were simply thrown out of the hatches. Communist guerrillas, ironically armed by the British to fight the Japanese during World War II, launched an attempt to take power. The emergency lasted until 1960 and involved a wide range of RAF operations including heavy bombing by Lincolns and ground attack by Spitfires and Beaufighters.

The Sunderlands were tasked to follow up after the heavy bomber raids, with their missions ranged against any survivors to break morale. These raids used smaller anti personnel bombs and strafing runs. Firedog missions were an ever-present feature of Sunderland operations from Seletar through the 1950s.

Further east, the Korean War required the Sunderlands to do the work for which they were designed - anti submarine and maritime patrols. While the first generation jets fought for air supremacy over the divided country, the Sunderlands from a much earlier generation of propeller driven aircraft were still searching vast areas of sea to enforce a shipping blockade.

The Tsushima Straits separated Korea from Japan and EJ155 was sent to Iwakuni via Kai Tak on 3rd March 1953.[14] Sorties were a mixture of weather reconnaissance flights

13 88 Squadron Operations Record Book ibid.

14 88 Squadron Operations Record Book ibid.

off the west coast of Korea, during which they were tracked by fighters from Communist China, and regular anti submarine and shipping patrols over the Tsushima Straits. Red Fox patrols were light shipping patrols to either side of the Korean peninsular in a bid to prevent supplies reaching the communist forces in the north. In 1953 EJ155 made three trips to Iwakuni for Korean war patrols. The war, in 1953, was in its final stages while the long negotiations to a ceasefire dragged on.

Back at Seletar a break from such duties was provided in April 1954 when the squadron were asked to provide an escort to the new Queen on her visit to Ceylon. Queen Elizabeth and the Duke of Edinburgh were travelling to the island onboard SS *Gothic*, with an escort of Royal Navy warships. After some hard work improvising spare parts, the squadron put up five Sunderlands which intercepted SS *Gothic* on schedule and performed a formation flypast for Her Majesty. The squadron flew patrols until they handed over to the Short Sealands of the Indian Navy.[15]

In September 1954, 88 Squadron was disbanded and then in January 1955 the two remaining squadrons were amalgamated to form 205/209 Squadron, still carrying out much the same duties.

On 21st February EJ155 was borrowed and taken to Borneo by another crew to bring the governor to Singapore. Landing in a swell off Tawau the port float was carried away and the propeller tips on number one engine were bent.

The aircraft was beached - without beaching gear - and an urgent order made for spares to be flown out from Seletar. Local residents not only helped with the work but also provided accommodation for the crews. The district officer was also reported to be very helpful and even loaned a labour force from the local jail. By 7th March repairs were complete and the aircraft made its return to Seletar to be returned to its usual crew. The aircraft was

Tawau Beach: EJ155 damaged and beached while repairs are undertaken on Borneo. Ian Fraser

15 88 Squadron Operations Record Book ibid.

Out to grass. ML797 (P) and DP198 (W) ashore for the last time at Seletar.

Bill Whiter

nicknamed "Tawau Beach" in memory of the incident, but the regular captain S/Ldr E W Beer refused to allow the name to be painted on the aircraft or even spoken aboard since, as he pointed out, it was pilot error which had led to the accident in the first place.

The other Windermere aircraft to see service in the Far East was DP198, which was first assigned to 209 Squadron at Seletar in August 1950. The next two and a half years saw little out of the ordinary. She was used on naval exercises with HMS *Kenya* and, based in China Bay, for shadowing and torpedo observation exercises with the combined Indian and Pakistan navies. Allocated to 205 Squadron on New Year's Day 1953, it was only four months before DP198 returned to Britain for a major overhaul. After a period with 201 Squadron at Pembroke Dock, DP198 arrived back at Seletar on 9th July 1957 for the final days' flying boat operations in the Royal Air Force.[16]

Assigned to 205/209 Squadron as "W" she undertook the normal flying boat duties, including operations over Malaya.

News of the gradual run down of flying boat operations came through in January 1958, a year after the last UK based squadrons had disbanded. It was not just the flying boats which were taken out of service. The facilities to maintain and service them were also reduced as S/Ldr Fred Weaver found when he took DP198 to the Maldives.

On 7th February he flew to China Bay in Ceylon to collect the Maldivian High Commission for a trip to Male in the Maldives. The Sunderland was refuelled by a bowser truck which had to drive out along a jetty to reach the Sunderland and even then extended hoses had to be used.

On landing at Male, after seeing their VIPs safely ashore, S/Ldr Weaver discovered an engine fault they could not diagnose. They managed the trip back to China Bay but, while sitting on the wing at the mooring, one of the crew noticed an exhaust valve sticking out of the exhaust on the engine. They needed a complete new engine.

Fortunately beaching gear was found in a dump in Colombo, and the refuelling truck was used to flatten down the jungle which was growing over the slipway and then to pull DP198 up onto the shore. It was also then parked in front of the wing to act as a platform to work from. The new engine was delivered by Hastings transport aircraft and was eventually fitted and test flown. But after 45 minutes airborne it was misfiring.

16 205/209 Squadron Operations Record Book AIR 27/2764. The National Archives.

Various repairs were tried but days were passing and still the engine could not be made to work. Eventually the cure was found when the magnetos from the old engine were re-used. The Sunderland finally returned to Seletar on 23rd February, over two weeks after they had set out.

Shortly afterwards 205/209 Squadron was reorganised as Shackletons, the replacement for the Sunderlands, were moved to Changi airport and the flying boats became known as the Sunderland Detachment.

In 1959 DP198 became one of the last two operational flying boats with the RAF and on 14th May DP198 was given the honour of the last operational flight by an RAF Sunderland, under the command of F/Lt Ben Ford. As part of Fessex 1, the exercise involved HMS *Caprice* and the flight lasted for exactly eight hours.

Navigator Bill Whiter's log book shows that the following day the last two Sunderlands, DP198 (W) and ML797 (P), made a farewell formation flight over Singapore Island. ML797 was to make the final Sunderland flight on 20th May with F/Lt Jack Poyser at the controls.

Plans to preserve one or both of these remarkable aircraft were mooted but nothing came of them, largely due to the lack of facilities on the long route back to the UK. At the end of the flying boat's days the only thing awaiting them was an appointment with a Chinese scrapman.

DP198, initially a Mk III Sunderland, had been accepted by the RAF at Wig Bay on 3rd November 1943 and served with 423 Squadron RCAF based at Castle Archdale in Northern Ireland. Post war she was converted to Mk V and joined the Far East Air Force with 209 Squadron and then 205 before returning to the UK for a spell with 201 Squadron at Pembroke Dock, becoming the last Sunderland to land on the Thames as part of the Battle of Britain week celebration in 1956. Then she was sent down the line again to the Far East for two final years of service at Singapore.

As other Sunderlands were withdrawn from use DP198 soldiered on, eventually becoming the longest serving of any Royal Air Force Sunderland.

What better tribute could there be for the workmanship of that small but proud band in their unique factory at Windermere?

The remains

A few years ago it was still quite easy to trace the remains of the factory at the White Cross Bay caravan park. Next to the club house, itself incorporating the old garage but since demolished, was a huge expanse of concrete which had been the foundations and floor of the detail shop. Following a path, which was clearly made from 50 year-old concrete, to the lake led to the discovery of another massive concrete pad, the base for the hangar.

Today even these traces have been covered over as the caravan site has modernised. The factory itself had been removed many years before by a Government which was encouraged to uphold their original commitment to remove the factory once the war was over.

The fact that many had found the best jobs of their lives at Short Brothers' Windermere works might have been one reason they were willing to battle to keep the factory open. But the campaign had a wider support from all sections of the community, in a curious reversal of the opinions expressed just four years before. Local councillors, the hoteliers association and the ordinary man on the street all added their voices having recognised that the benefits to the local economy and to people's lives was far greater than any harm originally feared.

A public meeting was called by the Calgarth Residents' Association on 31st January 1946 at St. Johns Room in Windermere[1] to highlight the strength of feeling, not just among former factory workers on the estate. The packed meeting voted unanimously for the factory to be retained as a productive unit by releasing it from the restrictive covenant.

The chairman of the meeting, Mr. H. A. Harrison, outlined the history of the site and said it was "beautiful in design and a happy place to work in". He added that it had not occurred to anybody that the factory would not be an eyesore when the government was urged to pledge its removal.

Chemical works: The Windermere hangar was bought by Albright and Wilson including and put to use on Merseyside as a chemical works. The building was heavily modified by Albright and Wilson inlcuding an extension to the front and massive 130 foot tower out through the roof as well as assorted pipe work and services.

Roy Perkins

---

1   Windermere move to retain factory, 2 Feb 1946, The Westmorland Gazette.

Secretary of the Calgarth Residents' Association, Mr. L. Douglas, said the factory was on trial for its life. He felt everybody should be concerned that, having cost so much to build, it should be put to good use. Local county councillors supported the retention including Mr. A. Hickling from Ambleside who said a board of trade representative had told him the factory could have been let many times over.

Mr. Hickling told the meeting: "Lake District people had not liked the idea of a factory in their midst when it was first broached but they had found it was not the smoky, dirty and unsightly affair they had believed it would be. They began to be attracted by it and it has offered opportunities for training and advancement that local people had not enjoyed before."

He added that he would like to see a small factory in every Lakeland village to implement a previous government undertaking to take work to the people.

The vote at the meeting had been unanimous only because secretary of the Friends of the Lake District, Rev. H. H. Symmonds had left before the end to make his way home. Asked about the unemployment of former servicemen in the district he had refused to be drawn into the discussion.

"The Friends of the Lake District regard the matter as closed," he said. "I will not enter into a debate at a meeting of which the purpose is to urge the Government to break its pledged word."

He did explain that the Friends had 2,000 members of whom half were local people and the society had the support not only of its members but other outdoor societies in their stance to test the government's intentions to restore rural England post war.

In London the government was well aware of the arguments.[2] Newspaper cuttings of the public meeting were in their files and ministers faced lobbying from several sides, including the prospective Labour candidate for Westmorland, Wing Commander J. C. McE. Gibb, based at Cark airfield.

The government had even been inundated with requests to use the buildings.

As early as October 1944, the Freshwater Biological Association, then based at Wray Castle, requested to take over part of the factory. Director Dr. E. B. Worthington said some of the smaller buildings might be suitable for the association. In June 1945 John Pattinson and Son Ltd. of Whitehaven asked if they could use the factory to store food but were told the buildings had not been declared redundant.

Even Short Brothers themselves expressed an interest in the buildings for post war production - but not at Windermere. The company asked the ministry if it were possible to move the hangar from Windermere to Rochester, where it was to have been originally. Short Brothers still wanted to build the Shetland and, with a prospect of an order, wanted to have the hangar at Rochester, and possibly the detail shop as well. In the end the Shetland orders never materialised and the need to move the hangar died with it.

The Ministry of Aircraft Production passed ownership of the site on to its successor, the Ministry of Supply[3] and it was decided to keep the factory for a time, but as a storage depot not as a manufacturing base. There were very few jobs in the depot for former workers but one man got the chance to return to White Cross Bay. Llew Llewellyn was put in charge of maintenance at the factory after Short Brothers had left.

The Ministry of Supply decided the 210,000 square feet of floor space at Windermere would be ideal for storage of some of the massive quantities of machinery and materials which were becoming surplus across the country. From across the north west, they were brought to Windermere.

2   Short Brothers Rochester and Bedford Ltd, local objections to the factory premises, Windermere. AVIA 15/3622 The National Archives.

3   Short Brothers Rochester and Bedford Ltd, local objections to the factory premises, ibid

The Calgarth Residents' Association.

22, Broadfield Road,
Windermere.
15th April, 1947.

The Friends of the Lake District,
 Pennington House,
 Ulverston,
 Lancs.

Dear Sirs,

It is understood that you are once again
pressing for the removal of the Calgarth Estate
'eyesore at Windermere.

At a time when the housing problem is
a major problem of the whole country do you not
think that your proposal is now hopelessly
impracticable and a blow at the men who fought
in the last war? To even think of destroying
about 230 bungalows, which means the homes of
at least 230 families, shows some misconception
of the country's present precarious financial
position.

If your Society devoted its efforts
and money to providing green paint for the
roofs of the bungalows, had them pebble-dashed
outside and screened from the road by a few
trees there would not then be an 'eyesore' but
a model country village where the children could
be brought up in God's fresh air.

We also understand that some of your
members are intending to visit Estate Residents
soon. If this is so we should be obliged if
members of our Committee could accompany your
representatives in order that a fair and
unbiased report of the interviews could be
recorded.

Yours faithfully,

Geo. L. Wrigley. Hon Sect.

*Campaign letter:
Calgarth Residents
Association letter to
Friends of the Lake
District, questioning
the call to remove the
village.*
**Cumbria Record
Office, Kendal**

Some of the first materials to arrive were aluminium sections from Distington that were used in prefabricated houses. They were stored in the detail shop while massive rolls of felt were stored in the office block. The heavy machinery, lathes, milling machines and other items which had been essential to the production of Sunderlands and the rest of Britain's war effort, were stacked in the hangar. Some of the lathes were of massive proportions. Their buyers were nearly all from the same source.

"A lot of the machinery came in from the Ruhr in Germany. Every now and then there was a sale but most of the buyers said it was a waste of time for them. There were two Russian buyers at every sale who bought nearly everything. There was a Cockney buyer who had made money from scrap in the Sahara, burnt out tanks and things after the war. He bought one of the lathes and gave me £5 to move a Herbert half inch chuck from another lathe onto the one he had bought. He said the Russians had spoilt the sales and made the bidding ridiculous," said Mr. Llewellyn.

Windermere had seen many big lorries bringing Sunderland wings to White Cross Bay but post war the narrow roads were filled with Scammel transporters moving in and out many tons of heavy machinery. A lot of the equipment came in heavy pine packing cases and many chicken sheds and gates were made from the crates.

The Friends of the Lake District had agreed to an extension of the time limit for the government to remove the factory and in March 1947 it was stated that the storage would be needed for one more year.[4] The factory provided 50 per cent of the storage needed by the Board of Trade and they were anxious to retain it for as long as possible.

However, by August 1947 plans were being drawn up for the demolition. Estimates placed the cost at £180,000 to clear the whole site after credits of £28,000 for those items which could be sold.[5] To just remove the hangar, dope shop, slipway and jetty would cost £105,000 after credits.

Removal team: A group of workmen pose in front of the part dismantled hangar during the removal of the buildings from White Cross Bay.
Valerie Hastie

4   Short Brothers Rochester and Bedford Ltd, local objections to the factory premises, ibid
5   Short Brothers Rochester and Bedford Ltd, local objections to the factory premises, ibid

A belated attempt to save it came from the depot manager A. E. Gollop who wrote to his bosses in Whitehall saying: "I repeat that this is a magnificent storage depot which we should retain indefinitely and hope to keep until it is demolished, if ever."

There were late attempts to buy the factory from the Ministry of Supply, including one customer who wanted to use it for boat building and storage. But by early 1948 the final hope had vanished. The Government undertaking to remove the buildings, but not the slipway or roads on the site, was carried out to the letter. The two main buildings were dismantled and removed and the rest of the site cleared apart from the garage near the entrance and the gatekeeper's cottage. All that remained were the concrete aprons of the foundations - up to eight feet thick in places.

It was certainly not the return to its original open field state the Friends of the Lake District wanted to see but the government had honoured their undertaking and a new use needed to be found. With tourism growing in the Lake District and more people owning private cars, in the 1950s the concrete aprons were found ideal for a caravan site.

Norman Parker, former Short Brothers chargehand, was brought back to White Cross Bay and his knowledge soon proved invaluable. When toilets were being installed he was able to pinpoint where the toilets had been in the factory and the original plumbing was used. The site was landscaped and was regarded, in its day, as a model caravan site.

As caravanners launched boats down the wide slipway a few might have wondered about the origins of the wide expanses of concrete but, by then, there was little left to show how White Cross Bay had played it part in the nation's defence.

But what of the buildings? With plenty of life left in the steelwork to offset the cost of demolition, the factory buildings were all sold. The office block reportedly went to K Shoes in Kendal, rebuilt on Natland Road and only demolished in the early years of the new 21st Century.

The detail shop, conversely, survived. It can be found not far from the A1/A69 junction at Newcastle - full of buses.

Newcastle Council wanted a new bus depot and in June 1949 approval was given for the acquisition of land at Slatyford Lane for the depot.[6] The Transport and Electricity Committee had scaled their plans down slightly because of national restrictions on capital expenditure. To meet their requirements, the council negotiated with the Minister of Works to buy what was described as an aircraft hangar from Windermere. This was, in reality, the detail shop.

"The re-erection of this building on the Slatyford Lane site will for the time being relieve the acute congestion at other depots and also enable vehicles to be properly housed. At the present time many vehicles

Old concrete: In the mid 1990s all the original concrete roads were still clearly visible. The concrete here has since been covered with landscaping and timber lodges.

Allan King

Bus depot: The former detail shop moved from Windermere to Slatyford Lane in Newcastle where it was put to a new use as a bus depot.

Allan King

---

6   Transport and Electricity Committee minutes, 20 July 1949, Newcastle Council.

Caravan holidays: Taken in the 1950s, this is one of the first caravans to use the new site at White Cross Bay.

Norman Parker

have to be kept standing in the open air," the committee was told.

The committee agreed to buy the building for £9,500 as it stood at White Cross Bay. The dismantling, transport and re-erection at Slatyford Lane was far more expensive. The lowest tender was from Walter Few and Sons of London who bid £20,615 to do the work. A further £1,000 was set aside to cover architect's fees and the cost of supervision of the project.

The work progressed quickly and in September 1950 the council was told the work was practically complete.

"The next and final stage will consist of the clothing of the structure, the erection of administration quarters and workshops and completion of the depot," The depot has stood up well to nearly 60 years of use and is still being used as a bus depot today. [see photo]

But what had happened the hangar, once the largest single span building in the country? Rumours abounded that it had gone to Speke Airport in Merseyside but they proved groundless. Then the answer came in a surprising letter from a former flying boat pilot now living in Canada. Alistair Limpitlaw had been a newly graduated engineer when in 1950 he was given his first assignment to oversee the dismantling of the lakeshore hangar. A former flying boat pilot trained at Pensacola, he moved onto fly Liberators in Ceylon.

The operation to take down the hangar was almost as big as the one which had put it by the lake in the first place. Alistair explained that the structural consultant on the project was Bylander and Waddell and the contractor used for the dismantling and re-erection was Carter Horsley of Whitehaven.

"I became involved in local politics over the project: the local population, to a man, wanted to keep the factory to help create jobs for locals. The Friends of the Lake District wanted it moved. Few of the members of that body lived in the Lake District at that time and though I disagreed with their philosophy, they were my project allies," he explained.

Dismantling was one thing but once down the steelwork for the building proved to be a logistical nightmare to transport. It was solved thanks to British Rail who also apparently turned it into something of a publicity exercise. The work started early in 1951 and was completed in 1952, costing considerably more to move and rebuild the hangar than it had cost to buy it from the government.

The new owners were Albright and Wilson, who converted the hangar to house a new chemical works at Kirkby. The rebuilding involved the same techniques as for the original construction ten years before. Three temporary props were set up under the main trusses while they were built. There was a built-in camber so that, once the props were removed, the deflection made the underside of the trusses level.

The hangar was refitted as a chemical process building. Roy Perkins worked for Albright and Wilson and recalled the building having an acid making plant and a tri-polyphosphate plant that made the phosphate powders used in the soap industry. The phosphates were sold to Lever Brothers to add to detergents. The dryers in the building sent steam high into the roof, carrying with it powders which made the rails for the overhead cranes too slippery to work. When they were needed the cranes had to be winched into position.

Albright and Wilson closed the factory in 1980 and, not long afterwards, it was decided the building had no future. The chemical atmosphere had taken its toll of the steelwork and, what was once Europe's largest single span building and the planned home for the failed Shetland flying boat project, was cut up for scrap.

Once the factory had left White Cross Bay, the opponents then turned their attention to Calgarth Village and called for its removal. The problem was that it still had a use.

The pledge to remove the houses was cleverly worded by a far sighted civil servant and stated: "as soon the Ministry of Health was satisfied that the housing needs of other parts of the country no longer made it advisable to retain this temporary housing accommodation in the Lake District"[7] But that did not stop the Friends of the Lake District insisting on their removal.

In July 1945 the Ministry of Supply was told 118 of the bungalows were occupied by Short Brothers employees still working at White Cross Bay. Another 80 were occupied by people on the recommendation of the council and the other two were empty waiting for repair. Such was the shortage of housing in Windermere immediately after the war that there was a waiting list of 55 people wanting to move onto the Calgarth estate which was gradually taken over by the Windermere council.

And then the hostel accommodation also found new residents.

One recent visitor to Windermere was one of those who lived for just a few months at Calgarth – one of the happiest memories of his life. Smartly dressed with a polite and welcoming manner, Mayer Hersh spoke with a still noticeable trace of an eastern European accent. In a remarkably objective way what he spoke about was surviving Auschwitz and the Holocaust and being brought to Britain as a refugee.

Part of a group of children rescued by the Jewish Refugee Committee, he was flown in an RAF Short Stirling to Carlisle and driven in an army lorry to Windermere where he and his young colleagues could not believe what was waiting for them. Each had a cubicle containing a bed with clean sheets and a locker for their possessions. They had no possessions but they had lockers.

Mayer was brought up in Sieradz in Poland, a region where, ironically, if he had not been Jewish, he would have been classed an ethnic German.

He was taken from his home when he was 13 and spent time in nine separate camps, including 18 months in Auschwitz Number 2. As the Soviets approached, he was taken to Stuttgart on cattle trucks to another camp where he spent the hard winter of 1944/45 working in a stone quarry. There were 600 in the camp but the survival rate was dreadful. By the end of the war only four were left alive. Mayer was by then 18. Liberated from the Theresienstadt camp by the Soviets he simply lied about his age when the Jewish Refugee Committee were looking for 1000 children to take to Britain. In the end they only found 732, including the many who had declared the wrong age.

Listening to a man such as Mayer speak creates a fascination with how anybody can survive, and what in his character enabled him to endure such horrors. Is it his obvious intelligence, is he particularly strong willed or cunning or is he perhaps simply lucky? But the reason why Mayer survived eludes even him. He says that it is perhaps a subconscious desire to live that kept him going – one he only became aware of later. He knows many other Holocaust survivors and, as with most groups of people with a single common bond, they are all very different people.

It is his objectiveness and lack of strong emotions that are particularly striking. He does allow himself one strong emotion – a huge gratitude for the people of Windermere for presenting him with not just freedom, but freedom in such a beautiful setting. He describes the overwhelming joy of what to anybody else would be a spartan lifestyle in Calgarth.

Walking round the fields at Calgarth today with him he explains that when he celebrated his 80th birthday he realised he had not expected to reach 17. He smiles and looks at the views, trying to remember where buildings might have been. But his mind does not

---

7   Short Brothers Rochester and Bedford Ltd, local objections to the factory premises, ibid

contain the map of where he lived. It holds instead memories of the joy of going over to the canteen for meals, of walking from Calgarth to Bowness and of sitting by the lake, dabbling his feet in the water and taking a boat out on the lake. Simple pleasures but an intense joy still tangible in his words 60 years later.

While at Calgarth, the boys were taught English, given medical checks and given the foundations for a future life in Britain. From November 1945 they left Calgarth for the next stage in their new lives. Mayer chose Manchester because his friends were going there. The Jewish Refugee Committee ensured they were not a burden on the state by continuing to support them until they were able to earn their own living. He took several jobs eventually working for a tailor and later setting up his own business in the town centre – the shop closing when the area was redeveloped for the Arndale Centre.

And now he tells his story to schools, to those who will listen, supporting the work of Holocaust survivors in the hope that the past is not forgotten..

The hospital at Calgarth had been used for first aid provision for the factory. After the Holocaust survivors left it became derelict until in the 1950s Angus McKay took it over as the headquarters for the reformed Windermere ATC.

While the Friends of the Lake District tried to get the village demolished, the Calgarth Residents' Association suggested they should direct their efforts more productively towards getting some green paint for the houses and some trees to screen the site and make it "a model village and not an eyesore".[8]

With prefabs being used across the country as emergency housing, it was inevitable that Calgarth should be retained despite the poor standard of many of the bungalows.

The hostels had been converted by the council to provide 44 new units in addition to the 200 bungalows, and all were rented out through the council's housing department.

The idea of building more permanent replacements was quickly seen as the answer, although the Friends of the Lake District again intervened and said new houses should only be built for Calgarth residents who had been in the area prior to the war.

Philip Cleave, secretary of the Friends, proposed "progressive evacuation" of the Calgarth houses with sufficient new houses built at Windermere "to hold all genuine cases of pre-war residents who are settled at Calgarth." He did not suggest what should be done with others who were moved to the area to set up the factory.

Awaiting demolition: One of the last bungalows at Calgarth stands alone waiting its turn to be demolished.

Les Riches

8   Calgarth Residents Association, 15 April 1947, letter to Friends of the Lake District, in WDSO 117 - boxes 32 and 33 Cumbria Record Office.

It was not until December 1950 that the Windermere council settled on the Droomer area of Windermere for their new council estate. The Calgarth Residents' Association asked to be given a high priority for the new houses to allow the village to be finally removed.

Building work at Droomer was well underway by 1954 and in the same year progressive removal of the bungalows began. By 1956 only 57 houses were occupied with the number falling to 27 by 1958.[9] The Ministry of Works had agreed to pay for the removal of the houses and the roads, Calgarth Village's last eight houses were in the north west corner of the site and were still in use in 1961 but were soon empty and demolished.[10]

Plans for new uses of the land were discussed and the Lake District Planning Board agreed to allow only public buildings and only on one fifth of the land. A secondary school was the ideal solution, and in late 1965 the new Lakes School was opened.[11] The final traces of the place where factory workers had lived were gone from Troutbeck Bridge when the old school buildings were removed in the mid 1970s.

As Calgarth and the factory buildings were removed so it became forgotten over the years. Peversely a pair of bungalows from World War One have survived while all the buildings built in the next war were removed.

During the war secrecy had gone hand in hand with security and workers were encouraged never to talk about what they did for the war effort. The secrecy surrounding the Windermere flying boat factory had protected it from bombing during the war and post war led to it being almost forgotten. It was rarely spoken about and memories faded in the same way as the concrete roads at White Cross Bay slowly crumbled. Only among those who had worked at the unique factory did any thoughts of the efforts to make massive flying boats still linger on. Alongside were questions about what had happened to all those aircraft so carefully built at Windermere.

Caravan site: An aerial view of White Cross Bay in the mid 1990s shows clearly the foundations of the two main buildings which were, at that time, used for caravans and boat storage.

Allan King

9   Friends of the Lake District archives, in WDSO 117 - boxes 32 and 33 Cumbria Record Office.

10 Friends of the Lake District archives, ibid.

11 Friends of the Lake District archives, ibid.

Fragments

Taking a bus from the centre of Liverpool to the Knowlesly Industrial estate is a strange pilgrimage. It is a dismal place - typical of big industrial estates across Britain. There is nothing of architectural merit, very little attempt at any landscaping. There are just wide roads, poor signposting and an unexpectedly baffling one way system.

Over on the eastern side of the estate is Acornfield Road where the bus pulls up at an lonely stop on a rather quiet bit of road, a little way from Kodak's sprawling plant. There is a line of small trees behind a steel paling fence that marks the boundary of the industrial estate, but it is a odd place to get off a bus.

That boundary is only the current edge of the industrial estate. Nearby a gateway, heavily chained and padlocked, gives away the fact that there was once something beyond it. This was where one of the largest aircraft hangars in the country was moved after it was no longer wanted for building flying boats at Windermere. This was where workers manufactured the chemicals needed for soap powder before queuing patiently for the bus home.

The foundations at Kirkby are not as deep as at White Cross Bay, made clear by the scrubby birch trees which have pushed through and started to colonise in the 15 years since the factory was demolished. Just to the north is flat rough grassland which was once a football pitch.

Walking across that empty space there is a sense of being too late - again. Twice now this building, the hangar that made its workers proud to work there, has become surplus to requirements. But this time there was no saviour. Between the clumps of grass and scrubby trees there is a brown crunchy layer underfoot, with almost the same texture as biscuit crumbs. The crumb layer, a dark rusty colour, is steel, left by the machinery used to cut up the hangar. It lies in inch thick layers marking the spots where the hangar was turned to scrap.

Some older maps still show an outline of the building, and a walk across the expanse of concrete might send a fragment of steel skittering off into undergrowth, but otherwise it is all gone

In Windermere there is little visible today to tell the story of the region's aircraft industry. Parking up outside the swimming pool alongside the Lakes School at Troutbeck Bridge the original access road into the Calgarth Village is still there, running alongside the northern boundary of the school. But the road simply leads to fields and a couple of older lake shore properties. The school playing fields and, beyond them, another field where horses graze, give away nothing of their history.

In a field off to the north, there is the remains of a tumbledown, low brick-built wall. No higher than three feet, the wall is the remains of the coal store, once behind the hostels that formed part of the village. Beyond it, through a small belt of slender trees is a stream - Troutbeck itself. Here something curious can be noticed. The bank on the far side is perhaps five or six feet lower. The ground underfoot is very rough. Occasionally bits of rubble and bricks poke through the tree roots and one strangely curved section of corrugated iron suddenly reveals itself as a part of a World War II air raid shelter.

Is this where the village went? Literally swept to one side when better housing was provided to its tenants, and since forgotten.

And what remains at White Cross Bay?

The expanses of concrete which could be seen perhaps ten years ago are now hidden. As the edges of the wartime concrete crumbled it made the caravan site look old. So

45 YEARS ON
AND PAYING A FLYING VISIT

THE SUNDERLAND FLYING BOAT

A unique opportunity to see the last Sunderland in the world return "home" to Windermere, where flying boats were manufactured at White Cross Bay in 1945.

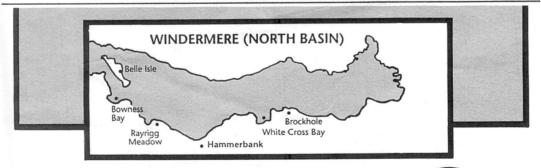

WINDERMERE (NORTH BASIN)

Belle Isle
Bowness Bay
Rayrigg Meadow
Hammerbank
Brockhole
White Cross Bay

Flying Boat on view Saturday 30th June - Saturday 14th July
For further information contact Derek Hurst (09662) 4502
or David Smith(09662) 2451
For information about cruises to the Flying Boat
Telephone: (09662) 6058 Bowness Bay Boating Co.
(09662) 3056 Windermere Iron Steamboat Co.

LAKE WINDERMERE FESTIVAL 1990

Poster sponsored and designed for South Lakeland District Leisure Services by Linear Design and Marketing, Kendal. Printed by Artline Print Ltd, Endmoor

the owners of White Cross Bay, wanting to keep the site up to date but unable to remove the eight feet thick foundations for the factory, chose instead to hide it. Hardcore and soil about three feet thick now cover the floor of the former detail shop and the hangar. On top of that have been built timber lodges, each with a tiny garden.

The paths and roadways to the lake have been tarmaced but still follow the same routes. By the lake where once speed boats were stored on the foundations of the hangar, are more timber lodges. The final section of the hangar was covered in the winter of 2005/06, the introduction of a speed limit on the lake having done away with the demand to store powerboats at White Cross Bay.

The slipway survives, still used for launching yachts which are moored to new jetties on the north side of the bay, not far from where the Sunderlands swung at their moorings. The old stone jetty where Sunderland II and Mussel were moored in the 1940s is still there, but are only used occasionally for landings.

Standing at the top of the slipway one only hears the sounds of children at play and boats clanking at their moorings. The hammering of rivet guns, the rattle of alloy plates and the roar of powerful aircraft engines are consigned to a ghostly memory.

Visiting these sites highlights better than anything else the way progress has eroded what physical remains were left behind by the wartime factory. The fragments left have become fewer and fewer, at the same time as memories have also faded. And while remains of the factory disappeared in the UK, so the aircraft themselves were disappearing around the world.

Originally only intended to have a short life, the Sunderlands lived on well into the post war era, still finding roles in a time when land planes became dominant. A bid to bring one of the last two Sunderlands home from Singapore - which could have saved DP198 – failed, not least because of the lack of servicing bases left on the long route to the UK.

The civilian airlines operating from the UK had stopped using flying boats a year earlier in 1958 when Aquila Airways closed its operations.[1]

Spares Source: NZ4109 ex DP191 in storage and being cannibalised for spares for other RNZAF Sunderlands.

1 Hull, Norman, 1994. Eagles Over Water: The story of Aquila Airways, Baron Birch. 0 860230547 5

The Royal New Zealand Air Force needed the flying boat's ability to land at remote Pacific Islands but, during the 1960s their fleet reached the end of its useable life despite several aircraft being broken for spares to keep the rest going.[2]

Those that had been operating in South America on the River Plate where the CAUSA and Dodero boats were based were finally beached in the late '60s and broken up in January 1967.[3]

In Australia, Ansett Airlines kept up a service to Lord Howe Island, between Australia and New Zealand, until 1974 when a runway was built on the island to allow land planes in. The two remaining flying boats aircraft were flown out to the Caribbean and eventually to the UK.[4]

Yet at Windermere one curious rumour of a survivor surfaced occasionally, told in whispers, about a Sunderland, possibly several, lying long forgotten on the bed of the lake.

It is an intriguing tale and an alluring one. Who would not want to find a Sunderland, complete and preserved in the dark fresh waters.

The prime candidates for being scuttled have to be the aircraft that were scrapped at Windermere, mostly during 1944. The first of these was W3983, a Mk III Sunderland from 10 Squadron sent to Windermere on 14th February 1944. Four days later it was classified as Cat E - a write off. It was not scrapped immediately but was assigned an RAF instructional number 4603M. It may have been used to show the differences between the Mk III and the earlier models or more likely just as an airframe for practicing repair techniques on. The aircraft was finally broken up on 16th June.[5]

Four other aircraft were scrapped at Windermere. W6030 from the Norwegian 330 Squadron was found to be too badly damaged for repair and was classed Cat E on 10th July 1944.[6] The other three were brought to Windermere after the RAF had them struck off charge, showing they were no longer in service. (see page 144)

So were any of these five aircraft sunk in the lake? It is not feasible, not least since, to a man, everybody who worked at the factory denies any aircraft were sunk in the lake. William Gerrish recalled watching one battered airframe being winched up the slipway before he set to work breaking it up with a fire axe. Alongside him working just outside the hangar, Bill Harrison also worked on reducing scrap aircraft to component parts.

"They created a big scrap pile by the detail shop. They carted the scrap off on a Lister truck and sorted into piles of steel and aluminium. We first lifted off the turrets and the radios etc would all be saved. A lot of it belonged to the ministry and not Shorts," he recalled.

An important consideration was the need for material in the war effort. Recycling was a necessity in the war. Indeed in May 1944 a directive was sent from the Ministry of Aircraft Production to all shadow factory managers which stated: "Retention of redundant jigs, tools and gauges absorbs valuable storage space and withholds from the war effort a substantial weight of steel and other materials."[7]

So if surplus aircraft were still valuable during the war, what about the situation after VE day when the large number of aircraft being scrapped led to massive surpluses of material. There are well recorded examples of surplus aircraft being dumped at sea and buried in quarries. Why not in Windermere as well?

In June 1945 all outstanding work at Windermere was cancelled. Only those aircraft on which work had already started were to be finished off. So far seven aircraft have been

2   Bowyer, Chaz, 1989. The Short Sunderland, Aston publications. 0 7110 0665 2

3   Barnes, C H, 1967. Shorts Aircraft since 1900, Putnam.

4   Smith, Peter, 1993. The Last Flying Boat, ML814 – Islander. Ensign Publications. 185455 083 7

5   A M Form 78, Aircraft movement card for W3983, RAF Museum.

6   A M Form 78, Aircraft movement card for W6030, RAF Museum.

7   Closing down or reduction of shadow factories: procedure, 1944-1945. AVIA 15 3825 The National Archives.

identified which were moored on the lake at the end of the war but were not repaired at Windermere. (see page 145) Could these surplus 'planes have been scrapped?

The records show that six were taken to other works and converted from Mk III to Mk V and went on to have post war careers.[8] The seventh aircraft was EJ151, which was built in Windermere and had returned home for conversion. The aircraft movement card shows EJ151 being ferried out to 57 MU at Wig Bay on 1st June and then struck off charge on 28th June. The aircraft was certainly scrapped but not at Windermere.

The idea of a conspiracy to keep stories of sunken Sunderlands secret do not make sense. With the wartime imperative to "Keep Mum" no longer necessary, the silence would have been broken by now. Peter Greetham the factory manager's son denies that aircraft were sunk - and he dumped a sign in the lake that announced that White Cross Bay was government property.

But if no aircraft were sunk then how did the rumours start? The first rumours I heard came from former aircrew. One crew member in particular believed his aircraft was left on Windermere to be sunk because that is what he was told by workers at the factory. Yet checking log books showed the aircraft was ML877. This went on to be the last aircraft converted at Windermere and went on to have a career with the French *Aeronavale*.[9]

Is it possible that the story was a joke told by a worker to tease visiting aircrew? Certainly the notion of a Sunderland being left on a mooring for a storm to sink it was much more interesting that being told about the refurbishment programme. With no reason to doubt what they were told so many years before, the rumour continued to spread.

Most recently there have been some tantalising tales of divers who have claimed to have found the sunken Sunderland, and a "sonar image" of one was even published in the press.[10] The sonar image has now been shown to be a poor fake and the divers have proved impossible to trace. But at least two groups of divers have searched the lake using some quite advanced modern technology. Tim Berry and his father Michael undertook a detailed search of the lake. Although much small debris was discovered, there was nothing even close to the size of a Sunderland.

Touchdown: Islander lands on Windermere - the last Sunderland to visit the lake.

Allan King

8   A M Form 78, Aircraft movement card for ML815, ML763, NJ171, DP199, ML784, EJ151 and ML783. RAF Museum
9   A M Form 78, Aircraft movement card for ML877. RAF Museum.
10   Sonar traces outline of legendary Windermere Flying Boat, The Times, 25 March 2004.

Like the Loch Ness monster, the story of Sunderlands in Windermere is an endearing tale, one easy to believe and hard to disprove. But these negative results cannot be ignored.

There is no Sunderland in Windermere. It is time to bury the story.

It is disappointing but there are no historical records to identify an aircraft likely to be there, everybody involved denies they were sunk and a good search of the lake drew a blank.

What is certain is that the last Sunderland to land on Windermere visited in 1990. By then Islander, the former ML814, was the last flying example of the breed in the world and came to Windermere thanks to one man. With an eye to history and a love of aircraft, the manager at the White Cross Bay caravan site at the time, Derek Hurst, was ideally placed to fulfil a dream and bring a Sunderland to the lake.

ML814 was not built at Windermere - that would have been too much to hope for. It came off the production lines in Belfast and had an active wartime career before joining the Royal New Zealand Air Force in 1952 for the start of a long and varied career in the Antipodes.[11] In 1963 Ansett Airlines bought NZ4108 from the RNZAF and converted it to a civilian passenger carrying aircraft but without the fully streamlined nose of a Shorts converted Sandringham. This unique civil Sunderland was christened Islander and led a long and eventful career flying to Lord Howe Island until 1974, when the land airport was built. Sold to Antilles Air Boats in the Caribbean she was eventually to pass into the hands of Edward Hulton who brought her back home to Britain.

Derek Hurst contacted him to ask him to bring the Sunderland from Calshot near Southampton to Windermere.

"Edward was very interested in bringing the boat up to Windermere. He wanted the aircraft moored on fresh water as a permanent home for it," said Mr. Hurst.

The visit was planned to coincide with the 1990 festival, after which it was hoped the Sunderland might be allowed to stay permanently on Windermere. The Lake District Special Planning Board (now the National Park Authority) gave special permission for it to land and the festival committee found the sponsorship needed.

For the first time in 45 years a Sunderland was to land on Windermere. Nobody realised just what a popular attraction it would be.

Lake wardens and police were out in force on 28th June 1990 to clear speed boats, yachts and other onlookers out of the way. No sooner was Islander on the water than a flotilla of light craft flocked out to greet her.

Islander was moored in Bowness Bay for the two week festival and then moved to White Cross Bay. Tourists were able to take trips out to see inside her and meet her crew. Then on 17th July Islander had to leave for Calshot. It had become clear there was no hope of a permanent home on Windermere. The authorities did not want a four engined flying boat on a lake busy with waterskiers and pleasure boats and there was no hangar ashore for her.

When Islander came to Windermere she had been up for sale. It took another two years before a buyer came forward. Kermit Weeks bought Islander for his Fantasy of Flight Museum in Florida, an aviation museum opened in 1995.

White Cross Bay: A view from the wing of the last Sunderland to be moored in White Cross Bay towards the slipway where new aircraft had been launched 45 years before.

Allan King

11 Smith, Peter, 1993. The Last Flying Boat, ML814 – Islander. Ensign Publications. 185455 083 7

*Last Remains:
Wreckage at the crash
site of DP197 during
the mid 1990s. Shows
the top of a fuel tank,
debris from the cockpit
area of the aircraft and
many small pieces.*

Allan King

The Sunderland was kept airworthy for a time and was even considered the flagship of the fleet. But more recently she has not flown and, although still considered potentially airworthy, the cost of putting her back in the air should not be underestimated.

The chances of her returning to Windermere, or even the UK, are remote. However, Islander is kept indoors, is potentially airworthy and is in good hands.

But what of the Windermere built aircraft? Sadly none have survived; some were lost in action, most were scrapped at the end of the war, and the rest broken up as they were gradually withdrawn from service

Apart from Islander, there are three Sunderlands in museums around the world and two Sandringhams. (see page 146) There are also two Short Solent flying boats preserved: actually quite a remarkable record compared with the poor survival rates for many other aircraft types.

But there is one place where just a tiny piece of the Windermere workmanship can be seen. In the far north of Scotland, the lonely and empty lands north of Inverness, can be found just a few pieces.

One of the RAF's Sunderland training squadrons, 4(C) OTU operated from Alness, north of Inverness and DP197 was one of the Sunderlands on charge with the unit. The Sunderland was the same one which, on detachment to Sullom Voe in May 1944 had attacked and damaged the submarine U-995 - ironically the U-boat preserved as a memorial in Germany.

On 15th August 1944 Sunderland S-Sugar - DP197 - crashed after being recalled from a night radar homing exercise with the loss of all the crew on board.[12] Because the weather was deteriorating, the Sunderland was recalled to base. It appears she was flying south following the Moray Firth coast when she drifted inland and crashed on high ground half an hour after midnight and bursting into flames. DP197 had been airborne for only an hour and a half and would have still carried a large amount of fuel when she crashed.

The accident record card states a very brief summary of the causes of the crash:

"The aircraft crashed into a hill and caught fire. The aircraft had been recalled owing to weather deterioration. The pilot was unsure of his position, failed to climb sufficiently to clear the high ground and failed to make use of radar and other aids. There was no evidence that any aids, radar, WT were used.

The weather was recorded as "Dark night with low cloud, rain and mist." There was also criticism of the way the recall signal was sent out without consulting the senior officer in charge and the station commanders were ordered to use flying control in the correct manner.

A salvage team from 56 MU were based near Inverness and would have been detailed to recover the crashed aircraft, removing large sections of the airframe to prevent it being repeatedly reported as a new crash site.[13] The bodies were recovered and 14 of the crew were buried at Rosskeen parish churchyard on the shores of the Cromarty Firth between the naval base at Invergordon and Alness.[14]

---

12 AM Form 1180, accident record card for DP197, 15-8-1944. RAF Museum.

13 56 Maintenance Unit Operations Record Book, 1940-1946 Air 29/1013. The National Archives.

14 Rosskeen Parish Churchyard Extensions. Commonwealth War Graves Commission. [http://www.cwgc.org retrieved 1 November 2007]

Nearly 60 years after the crash the hillside was still littered with small fragments, many recognisable as parts of a Sunderland. The team from 56 MU dealt with perhaps 50 crash sites each month and did not have time to clear them completely. As a result it is possible to find small sections of fuselage, some showing the pan headed rivets used at Windermere to help inexperienced riveters get a watertight seal. Stainless steel cables, expertly spliced by the lady with the long finger nails, are still shiny despite so long in the peat and control rods are still locked together with pieces of wire twisted securely by Jim Frearson on every aircraft.

Crash Debris: These small fragments in the peat of a Scottish mountain are the only surviving remains of the 35 aircraft built at Windermere.

Allan King

On one piece was even a faint trace of a name, a name scrawled inside the airframe by one of the young men or women at Windermere. There is no doubt this is their aircraft.

Standing there on a wet and lonely hillside so far from Windermere there is an eerie silence disturbed only by the wind blowing across the wreckage. Behind me the sun came out and a rainbow formed over the mountains of the Highlands. In front the waters of the Moray Firth were visible showing just how close to their track the aircraft must have been when the crash happened.

It is a fitting memorial to the men who died on board DP197. It is also the only physical remains of a flying boat built at Windermere during World War II.

Shepherded In: Lake wardens guiding Islander to her mooring on Windermere.

Allan King

Appendices

ABBREVIATIONS

Some of the commonly used abbreviations found in the book.

ACSEA	Air Command South East Asia
AID	Aeronautical Inspection Directorate
ARP	Air Raid Precautions
ASR	Air Sea Rescue
Asst	Assistant
ASV	Air to Surface Vessel (Radar)
ATC	Air Training Corps
(C) OTU	(Coastal) Operational Training Unit
CEMA	Council for the Encouragement of Music and the Arts
CRO	Civilian Repair Organisation
DFC	Distinguished Flying Cross
ENSA	Entertainments National Service Association
FBA	Franco British Aviation (Company)
FBSU	Flying Boat Service Unit
FBTS	Flying Boat Training Squadron
FEAF	Far East Air Force
F/Lt	Flight Lieutenant
F/O	Flying Officer
F/Sgt	Flight Sergeant
FTU	Ferry Training Unit
MAEE	Marine Aircraft Experimental Establishment
MAP	Ministry of Aircraft Production
MOS	Ministry of Supply
MU	Maintenance Unit
NCO	Non Commissioned Officer
OCU	Operational Conversion Unit
OTU	Operational Training Unit
RAF	Royal Air Force
RAAF	Royal Australian Air Force
RCAF	Royal Canadian Air Force
RNAS	Royal Naval Air Service or Royal naval Air Station
RNZAF	Royal New Zealand Air Force
RIW	Repair in Works
ROS	Repair on Site.
SAR	Search and Rescue
SEAAC	South East Asia Air Command
S/Ldr	Squadron leader
SOC	Struck off charge
Sqn	Squadron
W/Cdr	Wing Commander
W.Op/Air Gnr	Wireless Operator/Air Gunner
WT	Wireless Transmissions/Transmitter

RAF Aircraft damage categories

Aircraft damaged in battle or accidents were categorised according to the type of repair needed, whether or not it could be repaired by the unit or needed the attentions of an outside contractor. In 1952 the categories were changed and records of the long serving Sunderlands include the later system.

1941-1952	1952 onwards	Damage
Cat U	Cat 1	Undamaged
Cat A	Cat 2	Capable of ROS by the operating unit
Cat Ac	Cat 3	Capable of ROS by another unit or contractor.
Cat B	Cat 4	Repairable at MU or contractor's works.
Cat C	Cat 5 (gi)	Allocated as instructional airframe
Cat E	Cat 5	Write off

Cause of damage may be indicated by other notes:

FA   Flying accident
FB   Operational Loss
GA   Ground Accident
T   Technical Cause
EA   Enemy action

Sunderland Specification Mk III[1]

Dimensions:
Wingspan: 112 ft 9.5 in (34.39m)
Length: 85 ft 4 in (26m)
Height: 32 ft 10.5 in (10m) to top of fin.
Wing area: 1,487 sq. ft. (138 sq. m)
Engines:
Bristol Pegasus XVIII nine cylinder radial creating 1050hp max at takeoff.
Propeller: DH constant speed.
Weights:
Empty weight: 34,500 lb (15,000 kg)
Maximum weight (take off): 58,000 lbs (26,350 kg)
Maximum weight (landing): 52,000 lbs
Performance:
Maximum speed: 210 mph (336 km/h)
Maximum economical cruising: 178 mph (285 km/h)
Normal range in still air: 1,780 miles (2,848 km)
Overload range in still air: 2,900 miles (4,640 km)
Armament:
Eight 0.303 in machine-guns in three Fraser Nash turrets
Eight 250lb depth charges

---

1   Jane's All the World's Aircraft, 1945/46. Sampson, Low Marston and Company

Individual histories of the Windermere built Sunderlands

The Windermere built aircraft served in almost every theatre of the war where Sunderlands were used. The following are the main dates in each of their careers both with the RAF and other air forces and, in some cases, as civilian converted aircraft. The histories have been compiled from a variety of sources including the RAF movement cards, Squadron Operational Record Books and pilot's log books.

Sources:

* = Aircraft Movement Cards
** = Aircraft Crash Records
*** = Squadron Operation Record Books

DP176
28-9-42* Pembroke Dock
1-10-42 * 119 Squadron as D
25-12-42 First operation.
15-4-43 ** Crashed while on patrol over Bay of Biscay. The port outer propeller flew off and hit the inner propeller which also came off. The aircraft was ditched but dug in port wing and sank in four minutes. All crew except three made it into the dinghy and were found the next day by an RAF Catalina which directed a destroyer to pick them up.
Personnel Lost F/Lt Davies. F/O Waters. Sgt. Galloway
Crew rescued were: F/Lt J. V. Gibson. F/O K. R. Waters. F/Lt L. J. Davies. F/O P. R. McIntosh. F/O K. T. Every. P/O R. H. Tierney. Sgt. A. A. Thompson. Sgt. V. Lower. Sgt. T. Galloway. Sgt. H. T. French. Sgt. A. W. Parker. LAC E. Owen.
21-6-47* SOC

DP177
7-11-42* Pembroke Dock by 308 Ferry Training Unit.
31-12-42* 10 Squadron (RAAF) Mount Batten as F
31-12-42 To Gibraltar with VIP passengers.
6-1-43 Returned to Mount Batten with VIP passengers
8-1-43 Anti submarine patrol. Operational for rest of month.
17-1-43* Accident on flight from Mount Batten to Pembroke Dock. On landing bounced and tore off port float. The pilot misjudged his height in glassy water conditions when landing into the sun. ROS
3-2-43 U-boat attack. Sighted a U-boat 12 miles away and dropped two depth charges one minutes after the U-boat submerged. Nothing further was seen.
4-3-43* Accident. Landing at Pembroke Dock the starboard float collapsed after the pilot dipped the wing too much. He was checked for operations fatigue.
10-3-43 Back on operations.
29-4-43 U-boat attack. Saw a U-boat surfacing six miles away. Attacked and dropped six depth charges that straddled the U-boat. An oil streak was seen although the aircraft took hits from anti aircraft fire. Sunderland "P"/461 squadron attacked straddling the U-boat with depth charges which appeared to sink.
21-5-43 U-boat attack. A fully surfaced U-boat was sighted half a mile distant on the port bow. The U-boat submerged well before four depth charges were dropped and nothing further was seen.
2-8-43 Saw dinghy with 4-5 survivors. Circled until rescue arrived.
8-8-43 Ju88 Attack. On anti submarine patrol captain by F/Lt Gerrard. Sighted eight Ju88s, six of which attacked. The Sunderland jettisoned depth charges and was hit in the port mainplane and the port float but no members of the crew were injured. The enemy aircraft were thought to be hit but no positive evidence of damage was noticed. The Ju88s finally broke off the engagement and the patrol was continued.
August 1943 Had additional guns fitted to the galley and also four fixed .303 Browning guns in the nose of the aircraft.
11-8-43 Did not return from the patrol. Crew on board at the time were: F/Lt N. C. Gerrard, F/O K. D. Smith, F/O I. W. Bowen, P/O J. I. Rowland, A/Sgt D. Benningdon, A/Sgt W. E. Mathews, W/O F. Jones, W/O J. G. Webster, A/Sgt J. G. Dwyer, A/Sgt J. E. Challinor, A/Sgt J. R. Dallas, P/O P. J. Adams.
31-8-43 SOC

DP178
15-12-42* 1FBSU at Wig Bay
21-12-42* 422 at Oban as L
1-2-43 Ferried to Oban
3-3-43 First operation - convoy cover and active operationally.
15-4-43** Accident. Cat A. A tender hit the starboard wing float while manoeuvering.
9-6-43* 1FBSU
5-7-43* 422 Squadron
25-11-43* 1FBSU Wig Bay
15-1-44* 422 Squadron. Operational. Patrols in immediate approaches as enemy operating closer inshore
29-2-44 Accident Cat A. Collided with Sunderland DD853 while taxiying at Castle Archdale. The pilot attempted to swing away from the other aircraft but the engines cut.
18-5-44 Manned by a Norwegian crew, Last patrol with 422 squadron.

7-6-44* 330 Squadron of Royal Norwegian Air Force. Transferred from Castle Archdale. Designated L.

10-6-44*** First operation with 330 Anti submarine patrol.

6-7-44* 4(C)OTU as BA at Alness.

14-3-45** Missing. Aircraft on exercise from Alness in good weather when it simply disappeared with F/O McElloy and crew.

22-3-45* SOC

DP179

13-1-43* Pembroke Dock. Collected by 308 FTU.

30-1-43* 119 Sqn Pembroke Dock as V

23-2-43 First operation - Convoy escort.

29-3-43** Accident: airframe cat Ac engines cat B. Overshot a downwind landing at Mount Batten in rain and a 400 foot cloud base and ran ashore. The pilot was unfamiliar with Mount Batten and found himself inside Plymouth Sound with cloud on the hills and balloons on the breakwater. The hull was badly holed, a float torn off and aircraft submerged to main plane level. Salvage was by 10 Sqn personnel and National Fire Service. The aircraft was eventually beached on 31st.

12-8-43* 10 Sqn Mount Batten as M

21-8-43* First operation with the Squadron.

2-10-43 Failed to return. Airborne at 23.15 hours for patrol. At 07.47 hours a message was received at base stating that engine trouble had developed. Nothing further was received. Information from No. 10 group indicated that an aircraft had ditched 20 miles south of Scillies at 09.49 hours which may have been M/10.

Crew was: F/O F. J. Lees; F/O D. Anderson; F/O B. A. Binning; F/O J. B. Gleeson; A/Sgt. H. Goldham-Fussell; A/Sgt B. E. Stehr; Sgt P. L. Johnson; F/ Sgt J. R. Speirs; Sgt. W. H. Powis; F/Sgt. J. G. Lockney; Sgt. B. D. McDonnell.

31-10-43* SOC

DP180

2-2-43* Pembroke Dock.

7-3-43* 230 Sqn Pembroke Dock as O

7-4-43** Accident Cat A. Heavy landing in Gibraltar Bay, bounced and lost a wing float.

13-5-43*** Piloted by F/O Rand to Dar-es-Salaam via Mombasa. Others had used the same route.

7-6-43** Accident Cat A. In Aboutis Bay, Egypt. Landing close inshore the aircraft became grounded.

1-7-43 Arrived Middle East. Operational.

16-9-43 Returned to Dar-es-Salaam.

18-9-43 To Mombasa for Indian Ocean Islands tour. Route was to Diego Suarez, Mauritius, Diego Suarez, Seychelles, Mombasa and back to Dar-es-Salaam on 29th.

1-3-44 South East Asia Air Command.

2-3-44 To Koggala via Kisuma, Khartoum, Aden, Masira, Korangi Creek, Cochin and arrived Koggala on 11th.

5-3-44 SAR looking for survivors of torpedoed MV Fort McLeod. Saw wreckage and two lifeboats with 40 crew.

27-5-44 Operation River. Together with Q brought 537 casualties out of Burma, landing on Lake Indawgyi, behind Japanese lines. The last airlift of the operation was on 3rd July.

8-7-44 Returned to Red Hills Lake and then Koggala at end of Operation River.

29-1-45 Karangi Creek.

31-1-46* SOC by ACSEA

DP181

27-2-43* Wig Bay

7-3-43* 1FBSU

16-3-43* Assigned to 330 Sqn, no record of delivery

6-5-43*** First operation - convoy patrol 423 Sqn

10-5-43* 423 Sqn as U then D

4-7-43* 1FBSU

9-7-43* 423 Sqn

18-8-43* Castle Archdale.

11-11-43** Accident. Cat E. Returning from operation at 20.45, the aircraft bounced in a rough sea, the bow split open and the aircraft, which was heavily laden, sank. Court of Inquiry found that the pilot should have been informed of the sea state but also should have been prepared for a rough sea landing because of weather conditions. Four were killed in the crash and another died later of injuries. The rest of the crew (six) suffered slight injuries. Full crew list was: F/Lt M. D. Lee, P/O R. W. Hill, P/O L. R. Hobbs, P/O W. G. Arnold, P/O R. Hutchinson, Sgt G. S. Sheffield, F/Sgt W. D. Scott, P/O G. I. Raymond, W/O C. M. Hardcastle, Sgt J. F. Long, Sgt R. J. Green.

12-11-43 SOC

DP182

27-3-43 * 1FBSU Wig Bay

4-3-43* 204 Sqn West Africa as J

25-4-43*** Coastal Recce. J/204 operated from Bathurst, Jui and Freetown on anti submarine patrols and convoy escort.

May 1943 transferred to French 343 Sqn.

2-2-44 Accident. After engine failure was forced to ditch into the Atlantic and sank, although the crew were saved.

SOC

DP183
15-4-43* 1FBSU Wig Bay.
6-6-43* 330 Sqn Royal Norwegian Air Force. Oban as W
8-6-43*** Arrived from Stranraer.
3-7-43*** First operation - anti submarine patrol.
17-7-43* Squadron to Sullom Voe, Shetland.
12-9-43** Accident Cat AC. The ground crew put the chocks in place too early during a compass swing and
    the tail trolley collapsed.
22-9-43* ROS Short Brothers.
6-11-43* 330 Sqn.
17-2-44* Calshot Servicing Wing.
10-3-44* 330 Sqn.
20-3-44*** Missing. Anti submarine patrol. Failed to return. Cause unknown. Crew were Lt. A. Moe, Sgt H.
    Thue, Sgt P. Blytt, Qm K. Kleppe, Qm A. Berntsen, Qm A. Nodland, Qm O. Froystad, Qm H. Larsen, Qm
    H. Karlsen, Qm A. Johansen, Qm A. Jacobsen.
SOC

DP184
2-5-43* Wig Bay
6-6-43* 330 Sqn as F
8-6-43 Arrived from Stranraer.
22-6-43 First operation - anti submarine search.
2-7-43 Air sea rescue for a missing Beaufighter.
6-4-44* Servicing wing at Calshot
2-5-44* To Sullom Voe.
6-7-44* 4(C)OTU. Training duties.
24-9-44** Accident. Cat AC damage. ROS. At Alness rode over the mooring buoy and damaged the keel.
10-10-44* 4(C)OTU
15-3-45* Accident. Cat AC. ROS Short Brothers.
17-3-45* 4(C)OTU
18-6-45* 57 MU Wig Bay
12-7-45* SOC

DP185
21-5-43* 1FBSU Wig Bay.
8-7-43*** Transit Castle Archdale
12-7-43* 201 Sqn Castle Archdale as V.
13-7-43*** First operation - anti submarine patrol.
20-3-44* To Pembroke Dock 201 Sqn
28-4-44* 4(C)OTU at Alness.
3-5-44 On training flight found ditched aircraft.
22-5-44* ROS at Alness by Short Brothers
28-5-44* 4(C)OTU
25-3-45* Cat B.
31-5-45* 57 MU Re-cat E SOC
10-3-47* Sold to the Phoenix and Clifton Iron Works, Coatbridge, Scotland as scrap.

DP186
3-6-43* 1FBSU Wig Bay
19-7-43* 95 Sqn as J.
11-8-43 Acceptance test then ferried to Africa.
1-9-43* Arrived West Africa.
16-9-43*** First operation from Bathurst, Gambia.
27-11-43*** Detailed to locate and sweep the track of force FX containing the French cruiser "Jeanne D'Arc".
13-12-44*** SAR for D/95 (W6076) located in Dakar with engine trouble. Both returned to base safely.
Early June Transit back to the UK. Route was Bathurst to Port Etienne, to Gibraltar and then to Mount Batten.
    95 Sqn disbanded early June 45.
14-6-45* 57 MU
10-3-47* SOC Sold for scrap to Phoenix and Clifton Iron Works, Coatbridge, Scotland.

DP187
26-6-43* 1FBSU Wig Bay
12-8-43* 308 FTU
15-9-43* En route to French Squadron Overseas.
1-10-43* Arrived West Africa for French Naval Squadron.
The French operated Sunderlands under the First Flotilla and later under 7FE - the 7th GR Flotilla. The unit was
    under the RAF's West African command and given squadron number 343. Records for the squadron are
    not in the UK archives but they operated similar patrols to the RAF 95 and 204 sqns.
1945 Retained by the French Aeronavale.
Control of the aircraft passed to the French post war but it is unlikely that DP187 would have survived for long
    since Mk V Sunderlands were used post war.
1947 SOC

DP188

24-7-43* 1FBSU Wig Bay.

20-8-43* 204 Sqn in West Africa.

6-9-43* Accident. Cat AC. At Angle Bay near Pembroke Dock being taxyed down wind when it struck a buoy with the starboard wing.

8-9-43* 204 Sqn Pembroke Dock as L later C

17-10-43 Arrived in Africa having carried out coastal reconnaissance on route.

29-10-43 First operation - escort sortie.

April 45 Shortage of engines meant fewer flights made by 204 Sqn.

10-4-45 Final patrol flight.

19-6-45* 57 MU

10-3-47* Sold as scrap to Phoenix and Clifton Iron Works, Coatbridge, Scotland.

DP189

6-8-43* Wig Bay

12-8-43* 1FBSU

7-9-43* 230 Sqn as L. Flown to East Africa by the "scenic route" via the West African coast then across the continent to Mombasa and Dar-es-Salaam.

12-10-43* East Africa.

17-11-43*** First operation - search mission for Japanese seaplane thought to be from a submarine. Nothing seen.

March 44 To Koggala.

29-3-44** Accident. Cat A. At Kegli Island Base the keel was damaged by a submerged rock pinnacle in deep water but not marked on the chart.

1-4-44 South East Asia Air Command.

May to Dec 44 Mostly active.

29-12-44*** Patrol with no sightings. Last operation traced.

16-8-45* SOC

DP190

14-8-43* 1FBSU Wig Bay.

5-12-43* 270 Sqn as G.

5-1-44* Departed West Africa

11-1-44* Arrived West Africa

2-3-44*** First operation - escort patrol.

19-3-44*** ASR. Found and circled over the aircraft to lead a seaplane tender to the scene.

25-4-44*** First flight under 204 Squadron control - on loan as G

1-8-44 Flight from Lagos to Jui. Experienced engine trouble so diverted to Fishlake. Returned to Jui next day.

1-10-44*** Permanently with 204 Sqn as G.

25-4-45 Final recorded operation

21-6-45* SOC

DP191

The movement card includes a cat E accident on 11-11-43 that happened to DP181.

30-8-43* 1FBSU Wig Bay.

24-10-43* 423 Sqn Castle Archdale as 3-L

4-11-43 Collected from Wig Bay.

15-11-43 Moorings patrol

21-11-43 Convoy escort. Convoy SL139/MKS30 was attacked by a strong force of He177s and FW200s with radio controlled glider bombs. Along with DP191 was a Sunderland from 201 Sqn and Liberators from 224 Sqn.

Captain Mike Pearson harassed the German aircraft, using radar to intercept the raiders. The Sunderland was recalled one hour and 46 minutes after attack started.

(NB the ORB states that Sunderland W6007 was on this mission. Log books give the correct details)

21-5-44* Accident. Cat AC. At moorings hit by Sunderland DD847 which was taxying. ROS.

2-6-44* 423 squadron

29-7-44* 131 OTU Killadeas, Co. Fermanagh.

27-1-45 Frozen in on Lough in very heavy frost and damaged during thaw by strong winds. Cat AC. 8-2-45* ROS Short and Harland

21-3-46* 57 MU, in storage.

29-5-52* Cat 4RE - repaired Short and Harland.

17-6-53* Cat 4RE

19-6-53* To Royal New Zealand Air Force as NZ4109.

June/July 53 Ferried direct to Lauthala Bay in Fiji and allocated to No. 5 Sqn RNZAF as KN-C

29-7-53 First RNZAF flight - conversion training.

4/8-8-53 Search for missing vessel "Monique". Intercepted and shadowed HMAS *Sydney*.

Nov. 54 To Hobsonville for major inspection at TEAL. Returned Fiji Feb 1955.

19-7-55 Mercy mission to Fulanga. First Sunderland to land there.

26-8-55 Flew in salvage equipment for the rescue of NZ4111 at Nukunono. The aircraft had become stuck on an uncharted coral reef while taking off on 24th August. Beached and patched up NZ4111 was flown out on 12th September sporting the name, "Nukunono Baby".

7-10-55 Search for missing vessel "Joyita" with 25 passengers and crew bound for Fakaofa in the Tokelaus, 270 miles north of Samoa. 120,000 sq. miles of ocean were searched but nothing was seen. The Joyita's waterlogged hulk was found on 10th November but no sign of the 25 people on board. Radar tests showed the boat gave a very weak signal.

Dec 56 Hobsonville and into long term storage. Cannibalised for spares and sold for scrap in 1967.

DP192
3-10-43* RAF Wig Bay.
10-11-43* Issued to Australian squadrons.
11-11-43* RAAF Wig Bay.
27-1-44* RAAF Mount Batten.
15-2-44* Australian Government overseas.
Joined 40 Squadron RAAF as A26-6. The squadron was formed in March 1944 and based at Port Moresby operating transport flights to Townsville and Darwin. A26-6 collided with a wooden pylon used to mark the harbour entrance channel at Townsville while step taxying causing extensive damage. The Sunderland sank and more damage was caused by the tug which towed into the harbour. A26-6 was broken up at Townsville. The date of the accident is unknown.

DP193
3-10-43* RAF Wig Bay.
21-11-43* Assigned 201 Squadron, no record of delivery.
25-11-43* 1FBSU
1-12-43* 423 Squadron
8-1-44 Transit from Wig Bay to Castle Archdale and 423 Squadron.
14-1-44 Training flight - Circuit and landings.
25-2-44 First operation. Square search patrol.
10-3-44 Anti submarine sweep. Found about 40 survivors of a U-boat attack in dinghies. Left markers and reported position.
3-8-44* Calshot
6-9-44* 131 OTU
24/30-1-45 Damage to hull and floats when lough froze.
12-2-45* Repaired on site by Short and Harland
20-2-45* 131 OTU.
8-7-45* 272 MU
26-3-47* SOC scrap.

DP194
26-10-43* 1FBSU RAF Wig Bay.
6-12-43* 57 MU
30-1-44* 302 FTU
6-4-44* Depart for West Africa
15-4-44 Arrive West Africa
3-5-44*** With 95 Squadron as F. First operation - escort convoy SL157.
24-8-44 ASR for N/344, a French Wellington bomber. Nothing was found.
12-4-45** Accident. Cat A. At Bathurst, on landing the aircraft's nose dug in causing damage to the bows. The pilot had landed with the tail too high.
17-4-45 Back on operations - anti submarine patrol.
10-6-45 Transit back to the UK via Bathurst and Port Etienne.
21-6-45* SOC

DP195
6-11-43* Wig Bay.
8-1-44* 57 MU
25-1-44** Accident. Cat AC. Damaged by a gale at 57 MU's Wig Bay site. A total of 13 aircraft were damaged.
2-2-44* Repaired by Short Brothers working party.
14-2-44* 57 MU
Early 1944 transferred to 4(C)OTU.
20-5-44* Accident. Cat AC damage. No further details recorded.
21-4-46* 57 MU
11-8-47* 57 MU
22-1-48* Sold to Shorts, Belfast for civilian conversion. Converted to Civil Sunderland V with Uruguayan registration CX-AKR and sold to CAUSA.

DP196
22-11-43* 6 FBSU Calshot for mods.
14-1-44* 57 MU
16-2-44* 461 Squadron.
29-2-44 First operation - anti submarine patrol
18-3-44** Accident. Cat AC. Damaged at Mount Batten when hit a moored vessel with starboard wing.
17-6-44* 461 Squadron as K (in reserve)
16-9-44* 201 Squadron - (in reserve)
2-12-44 First operational flight
21-2-45 Investigated an oil slick. Saw smoke and suspected schnorkel but no contact.
19-4-45** Accident. Cat AC. Took off 05.54 on patrol. At 08.33 the starboard outer prop and reduction gear flew off. Jettisoned fuel and returned to base by 09.41.

23-5-45* 201 Squadron.
3-7-45* 57 MU
4-7-45* RAF Castle Archdale.
1-11-45* 272 MU
26-3-47* SOC Scrap

DP197
2-12-43* RAF Wig Bay.
20-1-44* 57 MU
30-3-44* 4(C)OTU Alness as S.
19-5-44 Transit to Sullom Voe for operational detachment.
21-5-44 Submarine attack. Operating from Sullom Voe and captained by P/O E. T. King, S 4(C)OTU attacked U-995, a type VIIc U-boat. The submarine was on its first operational cruise. Five crew members injured.
22-5-44 Returned to Alness
15-8-44** Accident. Cat E. All 15 crew were killed when the aircraft crashed into a hillside and caught fire. Recalled to Alness due to deteriorating weather, the pilot was reported to have been uncertain of his position and failed to climb sufficiently. The known members of the crew were: F/Sgt. Arthur Di Pesa (W. Op/Air Gnr); P/O Roderick William Fulton (W. Op/Air Gnr); W/O. Ronald Edward Jackson; Sgt Walter Komer (Air Gnr); W/O Leroy Hart Ludington (W. Op/Air Gnr); F/Lt. Robert Lyall Mercer (Pilot); F/Sgt. Reginald Cuffley Norton (Flight Mechanic/Air Gnr); F/O Ronald Shaw Rowson (Pilot); F/Lt. William Benedict Sargent (Navigator); P/O Vernon Cleveland Stordy (W. Op./Air Gnr); Sgt. Donald Roy Trask (Air Gnr); F/O Anton Nicholas Unser (Pilot); P/O Percy Alexander Whyte (Flight Engineer); F/O Thomas Benedict Wood (W. Op/Air Gnr).
SOC

DP198
3-12-43* RAF Wig Bay.
25-1-44** Accident. Cat AC. Damaged by gale along with 12 other aircraft.
19-7-44* Returned RAF Wig Bay
17-8-44* Calshot
24-8-44* Reserve Pool at Castle Archdale.
3-9-44* 423 Squadron as J
1-11-44 First operation - anti submarine patrol.
11-4-45* ROS Short and Harland.
21-4-45* 423 Squadron
10-5-45* Greenock SR
30-5-46* 57 MU. NB Conversion to MkV not recorded
1-7-49* Short and Harland for mods.
1-3-50* 57 MU
30-7-50* FEAF
29th July 1950 to 5th August - Ferry flight to Seletar, Singapore via Pembroke Dock; Malta GC; Fanara, Egypt; Bahrain; Corangi Creek, Karachi; Trincomalee, Ceylon; Seletar.
5-8-50* 209 Squadron as V and W
23-1-52 Air test with 205 Squadron
April 52 Detachment to China Bay for exercise with the combined Indian and Pakistan navies.
1-1-53* 205 Squadron FEAF as O
17-4-53 to the UK, route Seletar, Glugor, China Bay, Karangi Creek, Bathurst, Fanara, Malta, Pembroke Dock, Wig Bay.
29-4-53* FBSU storage
28-10-53* Short and Harland 4RE
11-3-55* FBSU Wig Bay.
2-5-56* 201 Squadron as A
Sept 56 Last aircraft to land on the Thames as part of Battle of Britain week.
29-6-56 To Marsaxlokk for "Fair Isle", anti submarine exercise.
21-7-56 Formal flypast at fete
31-1-57 Squadron disbandment parade but no flypast due to fuel restrictions.
11-2-57* FBSU Wig Bay
July 1957* FEAF
10-7-57* 205/209 Squadron as W
1-11-58 Unit known as 205 Squadron Sunderland detachment
14-4-59 Seletar to Glugor (Penang) Last Sunderland to land at Glugor.
14-5-59 Final operational exercise by an RAF Sunderland. Fesex 1 with HMS *Caprice*. The crew on the sortie were Wing Commander R. A. N. McCready (O. C. 205 Sqn), F/Lt. Ben Ford (Captain); F/Lt. Jack Poyser (Co-pilot); F/Sgt. Bill Whiter (Navigator); F/Sgt. Butch Tait (Navigator); M/Eng. Dickie Knott (engineer); F/Sgt. Bill Williams (Signaller); F/Sgt. Jock Armit (Signaller); F/Sgt. Ted Bevis (Engineer); F/Lt. Joe Josey (Signaller); M/Sig. Rocky Rochford (Signaller).
15-5-59 Final flight flown by Wing Commander McCready. A farewell formation flight over Singapore Island by DP198 (W) and ML797 (P). (ML797 performed the RAF's final Sunderland flight shortly afterwards.)
1-6-59* SOC Cat 5 (e)

DP199
4-1-44* RAF Wig Bay 57 MU
27-3-44* 461 Squadron as U. Transit to Pembroke Dock.
14-4-44 First operation - air sea rescue flight.

16-3-45** Accident. Cat AC. At Lough Erne hit a submerged object which tore off the float despite having landed correctly on the flare path.
14-4-45* 461 Squadron
27-4-45* Cat B Conversion Short Brothers Windermere - Cancelled
19-6-45* Short and Harland Belfast for conversion to Mk V.
13-9-45* 57 MU
19-8-47* Short and Harland for mods.
16-3-48* 57 MU.
20-5-48* 88 Squadron as C.
19-5-48 Arrived from UK.
18-3-49 Exercise with HMS *Belfast* including bombing exercises.
20-4-49 Chinese crisis. HMS **Amethyst** was damaged and aground in the Yangtse River. All squadron aircraft armed and on standby.
3-5-49 Delivered mail to the fleet at Alacrity anchorage off the mouth of the Yangtse.
16-5-49 Shanghai evacuation of British nationals. Brought out 38 passengers
5-8-49 Japanese cruise including landing at Sasebo and Iwakuni.
27-4-50 Rescue mission to HMS *Constance* to take off a sick rating.
12-5-50* 57 MU
25-5-50* Cat 4R Short and Harland
6-6-51* 57 MU (Renamed FBSU)
21-1-53* 3R by Shorts
11-3-53 Flown Belfast to Wig Bay.
7-7-53* FBSU
30-6-55* Sold scrap to BKL Alloys

DP200
14-1-44* 57 MU
24-3-44* 461 Squadron as X.
5-5-44 First operation - anti submarine patrol
8-8-44 Saw U-boat diving and passed contact on to a destroyer.
1-10-44 Accident Cat A - minor damage.
26-1-45* Short and Harland. Conversion to Mk V.
9-6-45* 423 Squadron - no flights recorded.
30-6-45* 4(C)OTU
9-2-45*** 272 MU Killadeas.
3-10-46* 57 MU.
30-1-52* Short and Harland 4RE with mods
27-6-52* FBSU Wig Bay.
11-2-54* 230 Squadron as Z.
15-2-54 Air test
14-5-54 Royal Yacht escort duties with F/Lt Bowater along with D-K flown by F/Sgt. Dillon from the FBTS.
31-7-54 Detachment evacuated the British North Greenland expedition from their base camp at Britannia Lake. Carried out a photo mosaic of 200 square mile area of Greenland.
11-8-54 Returned to Pembroke Dock.
20-5-55 Detachment to Seletar for Anzex One exercises.
18-12-56* FBSU Wig Bay
11-3-57* Transferred to non effective stock
4-10-57* Sold for scrap to International Alloys.

EJ149
10-2-44* Calshot for mods
5-3-44* 57 MU
29-4-44* 4(C)OTU as RR.
23-5-44 First training flight.
20-9-45* 272 MU at Killadeas.
end -11-46 All airworthy aircraft were flown out and the remaining were scrapped.
26-3-47* SOC Scrap

EJ150
6-3-44* 57 MU.
30-3-44* 201 Squadron as W.
24-4-44 First operation - antisubmarine patrol.
18-8-44 U-boat attack. Periscope sighted and six depth charge dropped across it. A large volume of compressed air bubbles erupted along with oil, paper and other debris. U-boat was U-107 which was sunk.
26-10-44 Squadron to Castle Archdale.
19-1-45** Accident. Cat AC. Taxying, the port inner engine cut out, the aircraft swung to port and the aircraft hit ML783 at mooring. Inquiry concluded that the Sunderland should have been towed from the mooring. ROS Short & Harland.
27-3-45* 201 Squadron.
14-5-45 Anti U-boat patrol - intercepted surrendering U-Boats
3-7-45* 57 MU Wig Bay.
31-10-45* 272 MU at Killadeas
23-3-47* SOC scrapped.

EJ151
23-3-44* 57 MU
6-4-44* 201 Squadron - no record of delivery.
20-4-44* 228 Squadron.
4-5-44 First operation - "special anti submarine patrol" at 200 feet.
11-11-44* 422 Squadron as H.
5-3-45 Anti U-boat patrol. Saw an oil slick and dropped a High Tea Pattern (Sono buoys) with a positive result. Surface vessels attacked.
11-3-45 Anti U-boat patrol. Assisted a Liberator and had a radar contact. Saw a swirl and wake 500 yards ahead and dropped markers but lost contact
3-5-45* Cat B Conversion at Shorts Windermere - CANCELLED.
3-6-45* 57 MU
23-6-45* SOC

EJ152
12-4-44* 57 MU Wig Bay.
3-5-44* 4(C)OTU, Alness, as TT.
17-5-44** Accident. Cat U - gun accident. One gun fired while being cleaned and killed an air gunner.
3-6-44 Anti submarine patrol off Norway. Attacked suspected U-boat contact but turned out to be a whale.
18-2-45** Accident. Cat A. At Alness, the port inner engine had a seized piston.
15-7-45* 57 MU
3-10-45* Saunders Roe at East Cowes
9-9-48* Sold to MOS (Ministry of Supply).

EJ153
10-5-44* 57 MU Wig Bay.
24-5-44* Servicing Wing, Calshot.
7-6-44 461 Squadron as S
17-6-44 First operation - anti U-boat patrol.
14-12-44* Recorded as Cat E but no record of any damage. Error on the aircraft movement card.
23-3-45 U-boat patrol. Saw periscope. No further contact no attack.
13-4-45* Short and Harland for conversion to Mk V.
4-7-45* 57 MU
24-5-48* Short and Harland for mods.
1-10-48* 57 MU
1-11-49* 235 OCU at Calshot as Q.
5-6-51** Accident 5C - recat 3R (on 21-6-51). On a low level practice bombing run, the aircraft struck high ground, slid along the hill and flew on with the hull badly damaged. On landing was beached on mudflats.
22-12-52* Short and Harland
23-12-52* Returned to 235 OCU.
24-8-53* Short and Harland 4RE
1-11-54* FBSU.
7-1-55* 230 Squadron as R.
18-5-55 Detachment to Seletar.
17-6-55 Submarine attack (simulated). On exercise saw a snorkeling submarine and bombed with smoke flares. The submarine was Russian and had been shadowing the exercises.
7-7-55 Returned home to Pembroke Dock.
30-10-56** Accident Cat 3R. Landing at Castle Archdale the aircraft struck a submerged rock which was not properly marked. The aircraft was later salvaged and beached.
1-11-56* FA Cat 3R
5-11-56* 278 MU 3R then recat 5(C) and scrapped.

EJ154
13-5-44* Wig Bay
24-5-44* Calshot servicing wing.
7-6-44* Pembroke Dock reserve.
31-7-44* 461 Squadron as T.
3-8-44 First operation - anti U-boat patrol.
8-8-44 Anti U-boat patrol. Illuminated a U-boat with flares.
13-8-44 U-boat attack. Had radar contact and saw, three quarters of a mile away, a U-boat fully surfaced. It opened fire and the aircraft returned fire and dropped six depth charges. The explosions enveloped the U-boat and silenced the flak. Some oil was seen and three escort vessels arrived which found some debris.
13-12-44** Accident. Cat E accident at Pembroke Dock. Landing at base collided with unlit marine craft which crossed the flare path. The aircraft was beached at Angle Bay. Later it foundered on the rocks becoming a total loss.
SOC

EJ155
2-6-44* Wig Bay
25-6-44* Calshot
11-7-44* 330 Squadron as O

20-7-44 First operation - U-boat attack. Attacked a fully surfaced U-boat. The depth charges enveloped the submarine which opened up flak forcing the aircraft to take evasive action. U-boat was still on an even keel but the decks were almost awash. Contact was lost. The U-boat was U-387 which was badly damaged.

25-1-45** Accident. Cat A. Overtaking a Northrop N3 in flight the Sunderland hit the Northrop's starboard float with its tail plane.

24-6-45* Short and Harland for conversion to Mk V standard.

6-7-45* 4(C)OTU

10-7-46* Wig Bay

8-2-52* Cat 4RE to Short and Harland for mods.

12-8-52* FBSU

18-11-52* Issued to the Far East Air Force.

1-12-52* 88 Squadron as D

1-12-52 Ferry flight to Gibraltar, engine trouble, finally to Seletar on 12-1-53.

March 1953 Korean war operations.

8-4-54 Royal Escort for SS Gothic carrying HM the Queen and the Duke of Edinburgh to Ceylon.

1-1-55* 205/209 Squadron.

21-2-55 Accident. Cat 3R. Landing at Tawau, Borneo to collect the governor, the port float was lost and No. 1 propeller tips were bent. The aircraft was beached and repaired with the aid of local workers.

9-3-55 cat 3(R)

23-4-55* 205/209 Squadron

16-11-55* FBSU Pembroke Dock

6-12-55* Cat 4 stock

4-10-57* Sold as scrap to International Alloys Ltd

EJ156

23-6-44* 57 MU

11-7-44* Calshot

25-7-44* 423 Squadron

7-8-44 First operation - anti submarine patrol

11-8-44** Accident Cat AC. Eight depth charges dropped from their racks to the aircraft's floor while testing. Damaged the floor and floor members of the aircraft. Caused by a faulty camera switch.

25-8-44* 423 Squadron.

8-9-44** Accident. Cat AC. A depth charge exploded on impact with the sea during a practice attack and caused damage.

13-4-45* 423 Squadron.

April to May 1945 - not used operationally with the squadron.

3-1-46 Sold to Short and Harland for civilian conversion. Became civil Sunderland V with registration G-AGWW and sold to Uruguayan airline, CAUSA.

EJ157

4-7-44* RAF Wig Bay.

22-7-44* Calshot

14-8-44* 423 Squadron as K

19-8-44 First operation - antisubmarine patrol.

1-1-45 U-boat Attack. Rear gunner saw orange object 11 miles astern. The object darkened and lengthened and then lost sight of it. Saw blue grey smoke, not drifting with wind. Dropped three depth charges and no further contact.

12-5-45* Accident Cat AC recat E. On take off the port inner engine appeared to be on fire. Forced landing was made. The exhaust housing had failed.

28-5-45* Recat E.

3-8-45* SOC

EJ158

2-8-44* 57 MU

24-8-44* Calshot.

9-9-44* 423 Squadron as M.

12-9-44 First operation, anti submarine sweep.

15-1-45** Accident Cat AC. On take off the starboard inner engine cut out causing the aircraft to hit one of the flare path buoys and tear off the wing float. ROS Short and Harland.

8-2-45* 423 Squadron.

19-5-45 Saw fully surfaced U-boat flying a blue surrender flag. Directed surface escorts to it. 10-6-45** Accident. Cat AC. Taxying on the step the rope holding the bridle and pennant broke at the shackle battering the hull causing leaks. ROS Short and Harland

28-6-45* 423 Squadron.

30-10-45* 272 MU

26-3-47* SOC Scrap.

Squadrons which operated
Windermere built Sunderlands

The Windermere built Sunderlands served with most of the RAF squadrons which were equipped with the aircraft as well as many of the overseas units which came under RAF control during the war. This listing, which includes ferry flights, training and maintenance units, shows the period of time each aircraft served with particular units.

Aircraft are listed with the identification letter given to them by the squadron, where known. The dates are when the aircraft was officially transferred to a unit which is not necessarily the same as the date it arrived at a base. Where transfer dates are not known, dates of arrival, or the first recorded use by a unit have been substituted. For wartime overseas units in particular the information on aircraft movement cards has several omissions but dates have been cross checked with squadron diaries to fill in gaps.

Squadrons			
10 SQN RAAF, Pembroke Dock			
DP177	RB-F	31-12-42 to 11-8-43	Missing in action
DP179	RB-M	12-8-43 to 3-10-43	Missing in action
88 SQN, Kai Tak, Hong Kong			
DP199	C	20-5-48 to 12-5-50	to 57 MU
EJ155	D	1-12-52 to 9-10-54	to 209 Sqn
95 SQN, Bathurst, West Africa			
DP186	J	19-7-43 to 14-6-45	to 57 MU
DP194	F	15-4-44 to 10-6-45	Return to UK and SOC
119 SQN, Pembroke Dock			
DP176	D	1-10-42 to 15-4-43	Crashed in Bay of Biscay
DP179	V	30-1-43 to 12-8-43	to 10 Sqn RAAF
201 SQN, Castle Archdale/Pembroke Dock			
DP185	NS-V	12-7-43 to 28-4-44	to 4(C)OTU
DP193		21-11-43 to 25-11-43	to 57 MU
DP196	NS-K	16-9-44 to 3-7-45	to 57 MU
DP198	201-A	2-5-56 to 11-2-57	to FBSU Wig Bay
EJ150	NS-W	30-3-44 to 3-7-45	to 57 MU
EJ151		6-4-44 to 20-4-44	to 228 Sqn
204 SQN, Bathurst, West Africa			
DP182	J	4-3-43 to May 1943	to 343 Sqn (French)
DP188	L + C	20-8-43 to 19-6-45	to 57 MU
DP190	G	1-10-44 to 21-6-45	SOC
205 SQN, Seletar			
DP198	O	1-1-53 to 29-4-53	to UK Wig Bay
209 SQN, Seletar .			
DP198	V & W	5-8-50 to 1-1-52	to 205 Sqn
EJ155	U	9-10-54 to 1-1-55	to 205/209 Sqn
205/209 SQN, Seletar			
DP198	W	10-7-57 to 30-6-59	SOC and scrapped
EJ155	U	1-1-55 to 13-11-55	to FBSU Wig Bay
228 SQN, Pembroke Dock			
EJ151		20-4-44 to 11-11-44	to 422 Sqn. RCAF

230 SQN, Dar-Es-Salaam/Koggala/Pembroke Dock			
DP180	O	7-3-43 to Early 1945	SOC
DP189	L	7-9-43 to 16-8-45	SOC
DP200	B-Z	11-2-54 to 15-12-56	to FBSU Wig Bay
EJ153	B-R	7-1-55 to 5-11-56	to 278 MU and scrapped

270 SQN, Apapa			
DP190	G	5-12-43 to 1-10-44	to 204 Sqn

330 SQN – Norwegian, Sullom Voe, Shetlands			
DP178	L	7-6-44 to 6-7-44	to 4 (C) OTU
DP181	U	16-3-43 to April 1943	to 423 Sqn. Not delivered to 330
DP183	W	6-6-43 to 20-3-44	Missing in action
DP184	F	6-6-43 to 6-7-44	to 4 (C) OTU
EJ155	O	11-7-44 to 6-7-45	to 4 (C) OTU

343 SQN - French Flottiles, Dakar			
DP182		May 1943 to 2-2-44	Ditched in Atlantic
DP187		15-9-43 to 1947?	SOC

422 SQN RCAF, Oban/Bowmore/St. Angelo/Castle Archdale/Pembroke Dock			
DP178	2-L	1-2-43 to 7-6-44	to 330 Sqn. (RNorAF)
EJ151	DG-H	11-11-44 to 3-5-45	To Windermere then to 57 MU

423 SQN RCAF, Oban/Castle Archdale			
DP181	U + D	6-5-43 to 11-11-43	Crashed at Castle Archdale
DP191	3-L	24-10-43 to 29-7-44	to 131 OTU
DP193		1-12-43 to 6-9-44	to 131 OTU
DP198	J	3-9-44 to August 1945	to 57 MU
DP200		9-6-45 to 30-6-45	to 4 (C) OTU
EJ156		25-7-44 to May 1945	to Shorts.Civil Conversion for Causa
EJ157	YI-K	14-8-44 to 28-5-45	Fire damaged. SOC
EJ158	YI-M	9-9-44 to 2-10-45	to 272 MU

461 SQN RAAF, Pembroke Dock			
DP196	U + K	16-2-44 to 16-9-44	to 201 Sqn
DP199	UT-U	27-3-44 to 27-4-45	to Windermere then to 57 MU
DP200	X + F	24-3-44 to 20-3-45	to 423 Sqn. RCAF
EJ153	S	17-6-44 to 13-4-45	to 57 MU
EJ154	T	7-6-44 to 13-12-44	Sank at Pembroke Dock. SOC

Training And Ferry Units			

4 (Coastal) OTU, Alness (Invergordon)			
DP178		6-7-44 to 14-3-45	Missing
DP184	A-G	6-7-44 to 18-6-45	to 57 MU
DP185		28-4-44 to 31-5-45	to 57 MU
DP195		20-5-44 to 21-4-46	to 57 MU
DP197	S	30-3-44 to 15-8-44	Crashed
EJ149	RR	29-4-44 to 24-9-45	to 272 MU
EJ152	TT	3-5-44 to 15-7-45	to 57 MU
EJ155		6-7-45 to 10-7-46	to 57 MU
DP200		30-6-45 to 11-2-46	to 272 MU

131 OTU Killadeas, N. Ireland			
DP191		29-7-44 to Mid 1945	to 57 MU
DP193		6-9-44 to 8-7-45	to 272 MU

235 OCU (Formerly 4 OTU), Calshot			
EJ153	D-Q	1-11-49 to 1-11-54	to FBSU
302 FTU, Oban/Killadeas			
DP194		30-1-44 to 6-4-44	to West Africa then 95 Sqn
308 FTU			
DP179		13-1-43 to 30-1-43	to 119 Sqn
DP187		12-8-43 to 15-9-43	to West Africa then to 343 Sqn
Maintenance And Servicing Units			
57 MU / 1 FBSU, Wig Bay			
DP178		15-12-42 to 1-2-43	to 422 Sqn. RCAF
DP181		27-2-43 to 16-3-43	to 330 Sqn. RNorAF
DP182		27-3-43 to 4-3-43	to 204 Sqn
DP183		15-4-43 to 6-6-43	to 330 Sqn. RNorAF
DP184		2-5-43 to 6-6-43	to 330 Sqn. RNorAF
		18-6-45 to 12-7-45	SOC
DP185		21-5-43 to 12-7-43	to 201 Sqn
		31-5-45 to 25-3-47	SOC scrap
DP186		3-6-43 to 19-7-43	to 95 Sqn
		14-6-45 to 25-2-47	SOC scrap
DP187		26-6-43 to 12-8-43	to 308 FTU
DP188		24-7-43 to 20-8-43	to 204 Sqn
		19-6-45 to 25-2-47	SOC scrap
DP189		6-8-43 to 7-9-43	to 230 Sqn
DP190		14-8-43 to 5-12-43	to 270 Sqn
DP191		30-8-43 to 24-10-43	to 423 Sqn. RCAF
		Mid. 1945 to 19-6-53	to RNZAF as NZ4109
DP192		3-10-43 to 10-11-43	to 40 Sqn RAAF as A26-6
DP193		3-10-43 to 21-11-43	to 201sqn. Probably not delivered
		25-11-43 to 1-12-43	to 423 Sqn. RCAF
DP194		26-10-43 to 30-1-44	to 302 FTU
DP195		6-11-43 to 20-5-44	to 4 (C) OTU
		21-4-46 to 22-1-48	to Shorts.Civil conversion for Causa
DP196		14-1-44 to 16-2-44	to 461 Sqn. RAAF
		3-7-45 to 1-11-45	to 272 MU
DP197		2-12-43 to 30-3-44	to 4 (C) OTU
DP198		3-12-43 to 3-9-44	to 423 Sqn. RCAF
		Aug. 1945 to 5-8-50	to 209 Sqn
		29-4-53 to 2-5-56	to 201 Sqn
		11-2-57 to 10-7-57	to 205/209 Sqn
DP199		4-1-44 to 27-3-44	to 461 Sqn. RAAF
		13-9-45 to 20-5-48	to 88 Sqn
		12-5-50 to 30-6-55	Sold for scrap
DP200		14-1-44 to 24-3-44	to 461 Sqn. RAAF
		3-10-46 to 11-2-54	to 230 Sqn
		15-12-56 to 4-10-57	Sold for scrap
EJ149		5-3-44 to 29-4-44	to 4 (C) OTU
EJ150		6-3-44 to 30-3-44	to 201sqn
		3-7-45 to 8-11-45	to 272 MU

EJ151		23-3-44 to 6-4-44	to 201 Sqn
		1-6-45 to 28-6-45	SOC
EJ152		12-4-44 to 3-5-44	to 4 (C) OTU
		15-7-45 to 5-10-45	to Saunders Roe then sold
EJ153		10-5-44 to 17-6-44	to 461 Sqn. RAAF
		4-7-45 to 1-11-49	to 235 OCU
		1-11-54 to 7-1-55	to 230 Sqn
EJ154		13-5-44 to 7-6-44	to 461 Sqn. RAAF
EJ155		2-6-44 to 11-7-44	to 330 Sqn. RNorAF
		10-7-46 to 1-12-52	to 88 Sqn
		13-11-55 to 4-10-57	Sold for scrap
EJ156		23-6-44 to 25-7-44	to 423 Sqn. RCAF
EJ157		4-7-44 to 14-8-44	to 423 Sqn. RCAF
EJ158		2-8-44 to 9-9-44	to 423 Sqn. RCAF
6 FBSU, Calshot			
DP196		22-11-43 to 14-1-44	to 57 MU
272 MU			
DP193		8-7-45 to 26-3-47	SOC and scrapped
DP196		1-11-45 to 26-3-47	SOC and scrapped
DP200		11-2-46 to 3-10-46	to 57 MU
EJ149		24-9-45 to 26-3-47	SOC and scrapped
EJ150		8-11-45 to 23-3-47	SOC and scrapped
EJ158		2-10-45 to 26-3-47	SOC and scrapped
278 MU, Castle Archdale			
EJ153		5-11-56	Cat 5 (write off) and SOC

VISITORS TO WHITE CROSS BAY

The details of the contracts to repair, modify and convert Sunderlands at White Cross Bay have not survived. However, the following, incomplete, list has been compiled from a variety of records, including RAF Sunderland movement cards, squadron records and crew log books. From workers recollections it is likely that 24 or 25 aircraft were repaired or converted at Windermere, although not all have yet been identified. The list also shows five others known to have been broken up for scrap.

The visitors are recorded in chronological order. Some "test flights" from Wig Bay were used as transit flights to pick up or drop off a crew. Where an aircraft was used on a transit flight to the lake it is likely that another Sunderland was either delivered for repair work or collected from White Cross Bay on the same day.

The author would welcome details of any flights to Windermere, by Sunderlands, Catalinas or other aircraft, not included on the list.

Date flown in	Aircraft serial	Unit or squadron	Purpose of flight
14-2-44	W3983	10 Sqn	For instructional use then scrapped.
28-2-44	DD860	201 Sqn	"For mods"
11-3-44	ML856	57 MU	"Test flight" to Windermere
11-3-44	ML856	57 MU	"Test flight" to Wig Bay
23-3-44	DD866	461 Sqn	Repair in works.

27-3-44	DD841(J)	4(C)OTU	Repair in works. Cat B MR
9-4-44	DV964	95 Sqn	Repair in works
9-4-44	ML764	57 MU	Collect DV964 crew
9-4-44	ML764	57 MU	"Test flight" to Wig Bay
14-4-44	DD834	228 Sqn	Repair in works Cat B MR
15-4-44	ML757	461 Sqn	Transit
5-5-44	W6059	57 MU	SOC. Scrapped at Windermere.
5-5-44	ML862	57 MU	"Test flight" to Wig Bay.
2-6-44	EK592	57 MU	Transit Wig Bay to Windermere
2-6-44	EJ155	57 MU	Transit Windermere to Wig Bay.
2-6-44	ML816	57 MU	"Test flight" to Windermere
2-6-44	ML816	57 MU	"Test flight" to Wig Bay
23-6-44	NJ178	57 MU	"Test flight" to Windermere
23-6-44	NJ178	57 MU	"Test flight" to Wig Bay.
23-6-44	EJ156	57 MU	Ferried out.
24-6-44	W6030	330 Sqn	Initially Cat B MR the recategorised as Cat E on 10-7-44 and scrapped.
7-7-44	W4024	10 Sqn	Repair in works - Cat B MR
17-7-44	ML872	57 MU	Repair in works.
17-7-44	NJ187	57 MU	Transit
26-7-44	N9044	4 (C)OTU	SOC and scrapped.
2-8-44	T9076	57 MU	SOC and scrapped.
2-8-44	EJ158	57 MU	Ferried out - possibly by T9076 crew?
15-8-44	W4037	57 MU	Repaired.
---9-44	ML777	461 Sqn	Weighed.
3-11-44	JM714	57 MU	Delivery to Windermere possible mods.
3-11-44 Catalina	JX247	57 MU	"Test flight" Windermere to Wig Bay.
11-1-45 Catalina	JX295	57 MU	"Test flight" to Windermere.
11-1-45 Catalina	JX295	57 MU	"Test flight" to Wig Bay.
17-1-45	PP137	57 MU	Converted from Mk III to Mk V
1-2-45	NJ176	422 Sqn	Converted from Mk III to Mk V
3-2-45	PP103	57 MU	"Test flight" to Windermere
3-2-45	PP103	57 MU	"Test flight" to Wig Bay.
4-2-45	ML821	422 Sqn	Converted from Mk III to Mk V
15-2-45	NJ191	228 Sqn	Converted from Mk III to Mk V
4-4-45	ML877 G	228 Sqn	Converted from Mk III to Mk V
4-4-45	NJ171 A	228 Sqn	to collect ML877 crew
5-4-45 Catalina	JX382	57 MU	"Test flight" to Windermere.
5-4-45 Catalina	JX382	57 MU	"Test flight" to Wig Bay.
10-5-45	ML813	201 Sqn	Overhaul. Not known if work was done.
Cancelled Contracts			
28-6-44	ML841		Cat AC repair - cancelled 15-9-44
28-3-45	ML815		Mk III to Mk V conversion cancelled 8-6-45
9-4-45	ML763		Mk III to Mk V conversion cancelled 8-6-45
13-4-45	NJ171		Mk III to Mk V conversion cancelled 8-6-45
27-4-45	DP199		Mk III to Mk V conversion cancelled 8-6-45
2-5-45	ML784		Mk III to Mk V conversion cancelled 8-6-45
2-5-45	EJ151		Mk III to Mk V conversion cancelled 8-6-45

16-5-45	ML783		Mk III to Mk V conversion cancelled 8-6-45
Other Aircraft			
13-1-45	Shetland prototype DX166		For weighing and centre of gravity tests.
Dec 1942	Short Scion G-AEZF		Operated as a landplane by Shorts as M-5 at No. 24 EFTS, Barton-le-Clay, in Bedfordshire. Was damaged in a gale on 4 December 1942 and taken to Windermere (by road) for repair. On 2 April 1943, repaired aircraft was sent to 24 EFTS, Sealand, Cheshire.
28-6-90	Sunderland G-BJHS/ML814 Islander		A commemorative visit by the last airworthy Sunderland. Arrived on 28th June 1990 for the Windermere Lake Festival. Sponsors of the visit were taken on a high speed taxi run along the lake on 30th June. "Islander" left Windermere on 17th July 1990.
27-6-94	Catalina G-BLSC		A commemorative visit by a Catalina, used by the RAF in a similar role to the Sunderland. At the time operated by Plane Sailing Air Displays. Landed on Windermere for the festival and departed on 11th July 1994.

SURVIVING SUNDERLANDS AND DERIVATIVES

IN MUSEUMS WORLDWIDE

Short Sunderland

The RAF Museum, Hendon, UK

ML824 - Sunderland MkV

After service with the French Navy, the Sunderland made her last flight in 1961 when she was ferried to Pembroke Dock to go on display at the former RAF base. After ten years out in the open, ML814 was dismantled and transported to Hendon for the new RAF Museum. The Sunderland is fully restored inside the museum and a walkway allows visitors inside the aircraft.

Imperial War Museum, Duxford, UK

ML796 - Sunderland MkV

Another of the Sunderlands operated by the French Navy post war, ML796 had a most unusual career. After service in West Africa, she was returned to France and put in store and then in 1965 was used as a nightclub and restaurant in northern France. In 1976 the Imperial War Museum acquired the aircraft and moved her to the Duxford museum for a long term restoration. She is now in the new Airspace hangar.

Museum of Transport and Technology, Auckland, New Zealand

SZ584/NZ4115 - Sunderland MkV

The aircraft is a Mark V Sunderland, part of a batch of 16 ordered by the Royal

New Zealand Air Force in 1952. It served with No. 5 Squadron RNZAF at Lauthala Bay, Fiji. The Sunderlands remained in service until 1967 when they were all sold as scrap except for NZ4108 which had been bought by Ansett (See ML814 below) and NZ4115 which was presented to the Auckland Museum of Transport and Technology where it remains on permanent display.

Fantasy of Flight, Polk City, Florida, USA
ML814/N814ML - Civil Sunderland V

The only remaining potentially airworthy Sunderland flying boat flew out of the UK in 1993 to join Kermitt Weeks' attraction in Florida. This is the aircraft that visited Windermere in 1990. It was part of the batch sold to the RNZAF and then sold to Ansett airlines where it was converted to civil passenger carrying configuration (although not the full Sandringham conversion) and named Islander. After a spell in the Caribbean with Antilles Air Boats, Islander was bought by Edward Hulton who brought her to the UK and carried out extensive work to keep the Sunderland airworthy. She was sold to Fantasy of Flight and, although not flown recently, is still capable of being returned to flight.

Short Sandringham

The Sandringham was a conversion of the Sunderland to a civil airliner which involved reprofiling the nose, replacing the tail section and other extensive rebuilding to remove military equipment and fit out the passenger cabins.

Solent Sky, Southampton, UK
JM715/Beachcomber - Sandringham IV

Converted to a Sandringham after the war, JM715 spent many years in New Zealand and Australia flying with Ansett as Beachcomber. Ferried back to the UK from the Carribean in 1980, the Atlantic crossing was the last flight for the aircraft which was bought by the Science Museum and made the centre piece of the Southampton Hall of Aviation - now named Solent Sky.

Musee de l'Air et l'Espace, Le Bourget, France
JM719/F-OBIP - Sandringham 7

Converted to a Sandringham from the Mark III Sunderland JM719, she began civil service with BOAC in 1947 with the registration G-AKCO and the name St. George. In 1954 was taken to Australia and renamed Frigate Bird III. Four years later she was sold to the French Company, Reseau Aerien Interinsulaire (RAI) and registered as F-OBIP. She continued flying until 1970 and then, in 1978 was rescued by the Musee de l'Air Du Bourget.

Short Solent

The planned Sunderland IV was to have a longer fuselage and stronger wings. It went into only limited service under a new name as the Short Seaford with a matching civil version - the Short Solent. The Solent shares a clear family resemblance with the Sunderland and the Sandringham.

Western Aerospace Museum, Oakland, USA
N9946F Solent III

This aircraft was originally built as the Seaford Mk.I, NJ203, later converted for civil use as Solent III, registered as G-AKNP to BOAC. She was owned for a time by Howard Hughes and is now preserved at Oakland, San Francisco.

Museum of Transport and Technology, Aukland, New Zealand.
ZK-AMO 'Aranui' Solent IV

Tasman Empire Airways Ltd operated services linking Australia with New Zealand and, later, to the remote islands of the South Pacific. ZK-AMO was built by Short and Harland in Belfast, became operational in 1949 and was retired in 1960, now preserved at MoTAT in New Zealand.

Bibliography

Very little has been written before about the association of Sunderland flying boats and Windermere. The following select bibliography gives a few ideas for further reading about Short Brothers and the Short Sunderland and the earlier aviation history of the Lake District.

1. Ashworth, Chris, 1992. RAF Coastal Command, 1936-1969, Patrick Stephens Ltd, 1 85260 345 3

2. Barnes, C H, 1967. Shorts Aircraft since 1900, Putnam.

3. Bowyer, Chaz, 1989. The Short Sunderland, Aston Publications, 0946627 34 7

4. Connon, Peter, 1982. In the Shadow of the Eagles Wing, The history of aviation in the Cumbria, Dumfries and Galloway Region 1825-1914, St Patrick's Press, 0 9508787 O X.

5. Connon, Peter, 1984. An Aeronautical history of the Cumbria, Dumfries and Galloway Region. Part 2: 1015 to 1930, St Patrick's Press, 0 9508287 1 8.

6. Coster, Graham, 2000. Corsairville, the lost domain of the Flying Boat. Viking. 0 670 86653 9

7. Delve, Ken, 2000. Short Sunderland, The Crowood Press, 1 86126 355 4

8. Evans, John, 1987. The Sunderland, Flying Boat Queen, Paterchurch Publications, 1870745 00 0

9. Evans, John, 2004. The Sunderland, Flying Boat Queen Volume Two, Paterchurch Publications, 1870745 03 5

10. Evans, John, 2004 The Sunderland, Flying Boat Queen Volume Three, Paterchurch Publications, 1870745 13 2

11. Hendrie, Andrew, 1994. Short Sunderland in World War II, Airlife, 185310 429 9

12. Pattinson, George H, 1981. The Great Age of Steam on Windermere, Windermere Nautical Trust. 0 907796 00 .

13. Smith, Peter, 1993. The Last Flying Boat, ML814 – Islander. Ensign Publications. 185455 083 7

Opposite: Calgarth Village: 200 bungalows, hostels for 300 people plus two corner shops and a school had to be built to accommodate some of the workers for the factory on land now occupied by the Lakes School at Troutbeck Bridge.   *Cumbria Record Office, Kendal*

Windermere Works: The entrance to the factory is at the top of this map, with the Hangar at the bottom. The Detail Shop, Offices and Canteen are close to the road.

Opposite: *Detail Shop: The stores are at the left of this map, with the electroplating room in the divide along the centre. The orange buildings around the edge are air raid shelters.*

Peter Greetham

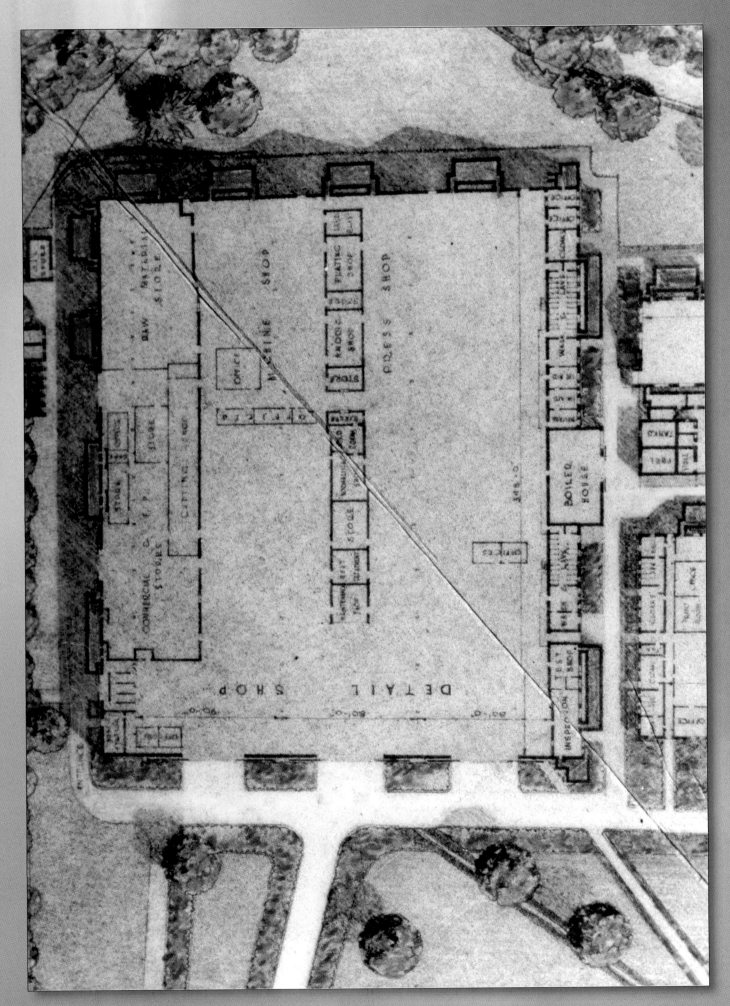

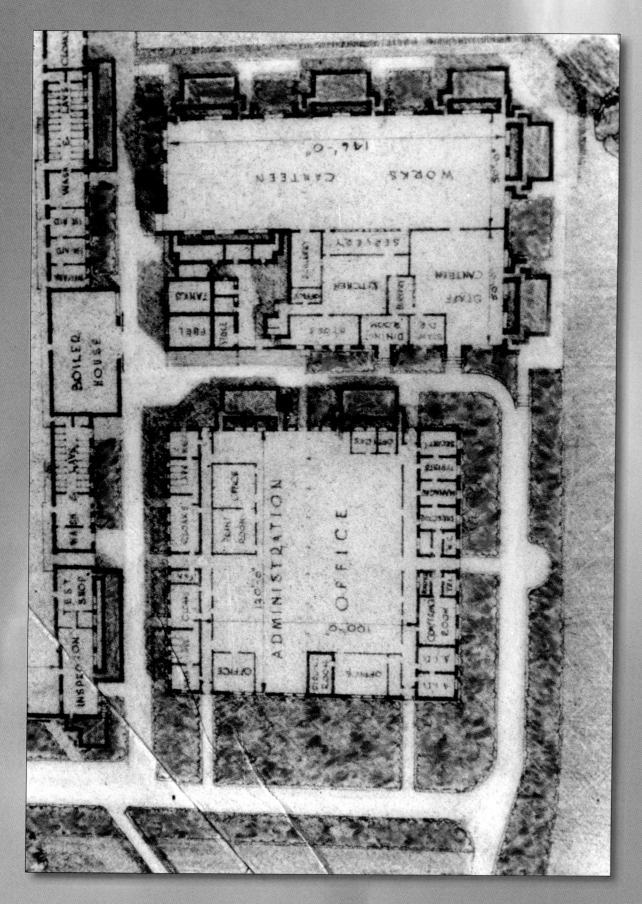

Office and Canteen: The administration offices had the senior managers' offices by the door leading to the canteen, which was divided into a staff and works canteen.

Peter Greetham

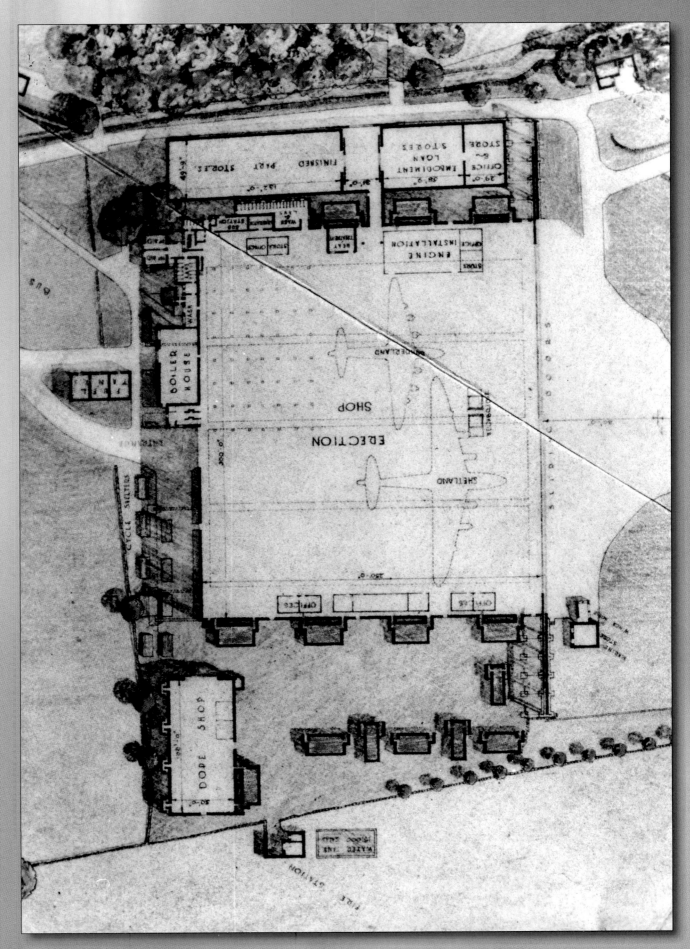

The Hangar: The plan shows outlines of the Sunderland and the proposed new Shetland flying boat as well as the jigs at the rear of the hangar. Alongside is the finished parts store with the Dope Shop separate on the far side.

Peter Greetham

Colour profiles

Short Shetland DX166 was the prototype and only military version of the Shetland built. It would have been built at Windermere if ordered.

A26-6 exDP192 served with 40 Squadron RAAF in an all over Foliage Green colour scheme until lost in an accident.

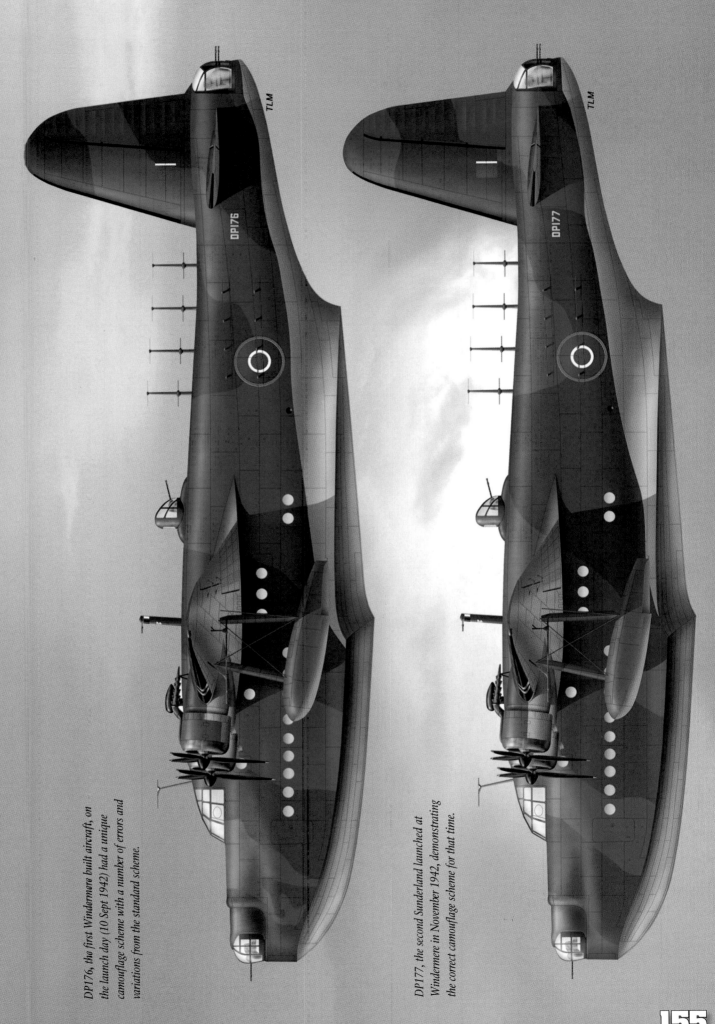

DP176, the first Windermere built aircraft, on the launch day (10 Sept 1942) had a unique camouflage scheme with a number of errors and variations from the standard scheme.

DP177, the second Sunderland launched at Windermere in November 1942, demonstrating the correct camouflage scheme for that time.

TLM

TLM

DP176

DP177

CX-AKR, ex DP195 was converted to civilian passenger carrying use and is seen at launch in the colours of Uruguayan airline CAUSA.

CX-AKR

DP180, serving with 230 Squadron in the Indian Ocean, shown in weather-worn SEAC camouflage colours carried in June 1944 during Operation River.

DP180

DP183, launched in April 1943, was the first Windermere aircraft in the new predominantly white camouflage scheme.

DP198, the longest serving RAF Sunderland, shown in the 1943 scheme as she emerged from the factory.

TLM

DP183

DP198

TLM

G-AGWW, ex EJ156, converted to passenger carrying use and shown as launched with a UK civil registration.

EJ150, shown in the 201 Squadron scheme worn by the aircraft when U-107 was successfully sunk in August 1944.

DP198, shown as W/205 Squadron, the scheme worn when the aircraft made the last operational sortie by an RAF Sunderland on 14 May 1959.

DP200, seen here as Z with 230 Squadron based at Pembroke Dock during 1954, the year the aircraft supported the British North Greenland Expedition.

159

EJ155, as U with the joint 205/209 Squadron based at Seletar, Singapore in 1955.

NZ4109, ex DP191, shown in the colours of 5 Squadron RNZAF during 1955.